DISTANT
THUNDER

DISTANT
THUNDER

A Helicopter Pilot's Letters from War in Iraq and Afghanistan

Don Harward

Grub Street | London

Published by
Grub Street
4 Rainham Close
London
SW11 6SS

Copyright © Grub Street 2012
Copyright text © Don Harward 2012
Copyright foreword © Charles L. (Chuck) Gant 2012

British Library Cataloguing in Publication Data

Distant thunder : a helicopter pilot's letters from war in
    Iraq and Afghanistan.
    1. Harward, Don—Correspondence. 2. Helicopter pilots—
    United States—Correspondence. 3. Afghan War, 2001- —
    Aerial operations, American—Sources. 4. Iraq War, 2003-
    —Aerial operations, American—Sources. 5. Afghan War,
    2001- —Personal narratives, American. 6. Iraq War, 2003-
    —Personal narratives, American.
    I. Title

ISBN-13: 978-1-908117-28-1

Cover design by Sarah Driver
Typeset by Sarah Driver
Edited by Sophie Campbell

Printed and bound by MPG Ltd, Bodmin, Cornwall

Grub Street Publishing only uses
FSC (Forest Stewardship Council) paper for its books.

CONTENTS

FOREWORD

It is a sincere privilege to be asked by my old friend Don Harward to write this foreword for his first publication. I am also very humbled, since I have not be in harm's way for many years and have the highest respect for those who serve our country day and night, on the farthest frontiers. I dare say *Distant Thunder* will bring back great and sometimes sad memories of when we were young and immortal! It certainly has for me.

In the spring of 1984 and while serving as the secretary to the general staff at the Army Aviation Center, Fort Rucker, Alabama, I was offered the opportunity to assess for a company command in the highly classified Task Force 160. Although well known today by virtue of its world-wide exploits, the military organization was then a very closed society; even within army aviation.

In June and prior to attending qualification training, I took command of A Company, TF160 from Major Frank Whitehead, an original plank-owner. If following a Nightstalker legend was not stressful enough, I still had to attend and graduate from the Green Platoon. For Don, myself and the other candidates, the PT, shooting, land navigation, and any other 'handy knowledge', like how to hotwire a car (I already knew how!) was easy. What was not so simple was learning to fly to the standards required of a Nightstalker. Thanks to the patience and determination of warriors like 'Flapper', 'Gumby', 'Guido', 'Snave', 'Snerd', Ranger Schwallie and others, we ultimately passed our check rides and joined the 'force.

In A Company, I inherited some of the finest young officers and NCOs our army has ever produced. Common characteristics of soldiers of this quality are patriotism, commitment, and total loyalty to each other and to our brothers on the ground. Today, like the author of this book, these men and women of our special operations forces are national treasures and we owe them a debt of gratitude.

Although Don went on to fly MH-47 Chinooks, instead of 'Little Birds', he always had that special look that I first saw in the eyes of scout pilots in Vietnam: fearless and bullet-proof. No doubt, he still does. CW4 (Ret) Don Harward is a trusted friend and someone I would be proud to fly wing. He continues to exemplify the warrior ethos and I wish him "Blue Skies and Tailwinds, Always!"

In conclusion, I found Don's letters an inspiring record of the dedication, faith, bond, and immense courage of himself and his comrades and would wholeheartedly recommend this volume.

Colonel Charles L. (Chuck) Gant,
US Army Retired 'Little Bird 6'

INTRODUCTION

I spent a lot of time thinking about how I might do this, writing letters about what I see here in Afghanistan, or what I saw in Iraq or in Panama. I want my children to know this side of their father and my wife to know this side of her husband; I want my friends to understand what I see and feel. I wasn't sure if, someday, these letters would take a different form. I thought perhaps they were meant just for me – a therapeutic medium to relieve pressure. All I knew was I wanted to do this, so here goes.

I hate labels and some are severely misused. One label that makes me cringe is that of hero. I am not one of those; I would never elevate myself to that place. No, heroes are much better than me. In my experience, heroes are sometimes found in cockpits, but not usually. However, I have served with some heroes in another world. They were guys who flew crazy missions who, frankly, America is lucky to have (or tragically, in too many cases, *was* lucky to *have* had). I love them dearly to this day and am proud to have served with them.

Real heroes are found in the dirt most of the time – like dirty firemen, or grunts (infantrymen) covered with filth after being unable to shower for a week. Or like the sweaty surgeon who I had lunch with last summer and who trembled as he tried to eat while telling me he had just lost another young man; he said he had lost quite a few. He told me how he had tried with all his skill but there simply wasn't enough to put back together; he looked so tired. I have prayed for him often, since.

Let me say first that, here, at least, I am simply a pilot. Back home, I hope I am considered a good husband, a decent father and an honest friend. I don't do anything extraordinary and I am nothing special; I am just an average, run-of-the-mill guy. However, on some occasions, I do see remarkable things. I serve with some extraordinary human beings and have been lucky enough to do so over a long military career. By the grace of God, and with permission from my loving wife, I continue on with this wacky, post-military – well, sort-of military, pseudo-military (whatever it is) – continuation of my flying career.

I would like to dedicate this book to all the warriors, some great and some un-known who walked off battlefields and to those who didn't. Those mighty men who so dearly loved freedom. May God keep them all in his comforting grace.

To Jody who I loved like a son, who loved his country more than his own life.

To my wife and family for having the love and understanding to let me go and do what I had to. And to all you nameless many who tirelessly prayed for my safety throughout all those years.

God, grant us the courage to face our enemies head-on. Bless our young warriors – and please bring as many of them home as possible.

Note to reader: The letters in this book were written about the battlefields of Panama, Iraq and Afghanistan during the years 1989 through 2010.

Chapter 1

FIRST LETTERS
FROM WAR

The other day after flying over the Red Desert at 300 feet for forty-five minutes, we were staring at the Helmand valley. The Red Desert is a strange geological feature with a vast area of red-coloured sand and endless dunes stretching to the horizon. It is relatively devoid of human life, except for a scattering of Bedouins, and therefore a safer place to fly. 300 feet is a luxury to a combat pilot; in Baghdad, we had to keep it locked on 115 feet. Lower and we might catch an antenna; higher and the people firing at us from the street had another second or two to take aim.

We made the most of the safety of the Red Desert because just outside of Kandahar, where I am based, a British Army Chinook was fired upon by a rocket-propelled grenade just as it left the traffic pattern. Just to the south of Kandahar, and on the other side of a small range of mountains that separates Kandahar City from the coalition airfield, is the Panjwai valley. The birthplace of the Taliban, the Panjwai valley has produced many American, Canadian and Taliban casualties. It is a sore spot for the Taliban in recent history; they want it back and we won't let them have it.

I wrote to my pastor about the utter evil I once felt while flying an escort mission over that place. I had been escorting a flight of helicopters with the gun bird. I decided to sprint ahead of the formation as they made their way towards a special forces' firebase to take up a CAP (combat air patrol) over the LZ (landing zone). As I circled overhead, looking for anything that might suggest an impending attack, it struck me as odd that there were no people; no kids running around, no women inside the walled courtyards, no men or boys tending the animals – nothing. At that moment, I felt as if total evil was looking up at me. I don't know why and I can't explain it, but my skin was crawling. Later, after we had left, a large enemy force attacked our guys and killed one brave American and wounded several more. There are always many more heinous injuries than deaths; the death toll is never the complete story. Can someone please tell me how we can afford the loss of these men?

The Panjwai valley sits on a wadi and forms the northern border of the Red Desert, which literally ends where it drops sharply to the wadi, 100 to 200 feet below. The Red Desert instantly changes colour to a light brown at the exact point where the wadi and the desert sand meet – strange indeed.

Further to the west, the Panjwai valley swings south and empties into the Helmand valley. This region is, or at least was, a major agricultural centre for food production. Today, around seventy-five percent of its area is planted in opium poppies, which are used for the production of heroin. This cash crop helps to finance terrorists while simultaneously ruining thousands of lives, and Afghanistan produces most of the heroin used on the planet.

The Helmand valley is full of enemy. There are several major operations currently taking place there. To the south lies Garmsir, where a fight is taking place, and to our north – in the Sangin valley, which is no more than a northern extension of the Helmand – the Taliban may actually control the countryside. Immediately north of our flight lay the city of Lashkar Gah, which has a coalition presence, and many Taliban fighters. On this day, just north of Lashkar Gah was a kill box – a no-fly area (for me) in which there was significant military activity.

The Sangin lies in the British sector (since I do not have to be politically correct in my musings here, I can speak the truth and not worry about whose sensitivities my writing might offend). The British are our strongest allies but their defence minister is not one to go looking for a fight. He has a politically correct, twenty-first century, one-size-fits-all attitude. He believes that any mission in which the British don't fire a shot is a success. All of which is lost on those of us over here who are fighting against a twelfth century people who only understand force. If they wanted to, the British could attack the area in force and dig out the insurgents. Instead, they stand off and lob an occasional bomb and perform limited direct contact military ops. Their soldiers have the heart for it, but their leaders lack the warrior spirit. So, for the time being, that area is essentially a no-fly area for me, or my chances of survival would be questionable.

This day's mission was to provide cover for ground forces. Who those forces were and what they were doing will have to remain a secret for the time being, but the mission was a good one and our targets were there. We always fly a minimum of two ships (Bell Super Huey IIs), at least one gunship and one CSAR (combat search and rescue) bird. The gunship is armed with twin GAU-17 mini guns, each capable of firing 3,000 rounds of 7.62 mm ammunition a minute. We carry a basic load of 4,400 rounds. A single 'burp' from one of these mini-guns sends a cloud of bullets toward the target. If we get the drop, they will not survive the next five seconds; they will die suddenly and violently, ripped apart by streams of high-speed projectiles. It sounds bad, I know, but so does the blowing to pieces of women and children by suicide bombers – something I have had the misfortune to see several times.

Our CSAR aircraft is a tactical version of a Life Flight domestic helicopter. However, unlike those more civilised helos, ours carries armour and extra fuel. Also a Super Huey, the SAR (search and rescue) bird is manned by two pilots and two SAR medics. The latter are special forces combat medics who go to ground carrying both advanced medical lifesaving equipment, and weapons – M4 carbines and M9 pistols. They must provide their own security on the ground while taking care of their patients. They, like the pilots, are all veterans of multiple combat tours and are consummate professionals.

On this day, I was flying the CSAR aircraft and was the AMC (air mission commander), and was fortunate enough to have a second gunship along for the day. The second gunship carried two gunners – one each side – manning a light (M240) machine gun in each door. We call bird with the 240s the 'light gun' and the GAU-armed bird, the 'heavy gun'. My job was to provide cover to ground operations throughout the day and to make all the tactical decisions as to how we would do that.

We went heavy this day because the previous day, our CSAR bird had been engaged by small-arms fire and a single RPG (rocket-propelled grenade), which, by the grace of God, missed. Our ground forces had also been attacked and fired upon during their withdrawal. We hadn't been able to retaliate because of the attackers' proximity to non-combatants. We saw them – we even photographed them! However, unlike the terrorists, we value human life highly and follow strict rules of engagement to protect it. I know that if I ever have to make the horrible decision to fire in order to save our guys when it may also destroy innocents, I will make it – but I pray I will never be called upon to do so.

We have increasingly come under a growing threat from surface-to-air shoulder-fired missiles that our allies are selling to the Taliban. Yes, that's right, our allies. If only the public knew the truth. Nations that agree to help us in our fight against the terrorists also secretly supply them with weapons and training. The politics sicken me with the constant lies and changing of the truth; thankfully, it is not my world. Mine is a world of instant decisions – good or bad, right or wrong, fight or flight, shoot, or save it for a better time. I like that world. I have found it to be a place where honour lives, where integrity counts, and where men and women stand up for what they believe in. It is a good place in the middle of an evil place.

Everything we do out here – even the occasional necessary 'physiological break' – has tactical considerations. When someone has to go, do I pull the one ship out of the area to a safe place in the nearby desert or send both ships out as a flight? If I leave one, then neither is covered, but if nothing has been going on and it is a 'peaceful' day, then maybe just sending one is OK. It's all a juggling act in which every move must be carefully thought out. When we return, do I approach the field site from the south or the west? South is where the enemy might be. However, we approached from the west the last time, so did they get a chance to put a heavy machine gun in there and are they just waiting for the next aircraft to fly by? Being predictable over here is a sure-fire way to get caught out, fast.

As the gunships maintained their patrol, I picked a good vantage point just across the Helmand river on a bluff overlooking the fields and farmland where they were patrolling a mile or two away. The locals were flashing us – flashing mirrors at our cockpits, trying to blind or distract us. They also use the mirrors to try to lure us in like anglers lure trophy bass with metallic spinners flashing through the water. At the wrong end of that mirror might be a hail of 7.62-mm fire or, if it was a really bad day, an RPG or a 12.7-mm Diska heavy machine gun.

We landed on the edge of that bluff. I was flying and Dick Edington was operating the radios. Our two CSAR medics alighted and began scanning with binoculars. On the cliff face just below where the aircraft rested, we noted three caves with signs of recent usage. Behind us, about two miles away, was a Bedouin tending his herd of goats. The spot looked good but not great, so I kept the bird at operating RPM so I could take off in a hurry if someone tried to drop a mortar round on us. I estimated us to be around 2,000 metres from the nearest walled village across the river – the only place from which a Chechnyan sniper might try to shoot at us. We were out of sight and out of range from anywhere else. Nevertheless, I am never able to relax while out in 'Indian country'.

As we sat and watched, the gunships did their thing throughout the day, eventually each logging nearly eight hours flight time for the day. As far as I know, not a shot was fired; it was a good day. We survived to fly another day and all our aircraft were reusable at the day's end. When we returned to base and I walked away from my helicopter wearing my heavy-armoured vest, and carrying my helmet and weapons, I turned to look back at our camouflaged Hueys. Funny, but all I could see were my wife and kids, and my home far away in Kentucky.

Chapter 2

BEING
TESTED

I think, from their earliest days as soldiers or aviators – although often those terms describe the same people – young men and women yearn to experience battle. They want to know what a bullet sounds like zipping by and to hear the crash of big guns. They want to sit in the middle of it and be tested. Will they fold or win a medal? Will they run for cover or search for a target? Are they 'man' enough (no chauvinism intended)?

I was no different than any other young fool and yearned for the same things. I wanted to get out there and be tested, to see if I had what my father had when he steadied his B-17 with flak bursting all around. Would I be good enough, could I measure up to others who had 'been there'? I am living proof that the good Lord forgives and protects fools. If it were not so, I wouldn't be writing this series of letters about my thoughts. I would have long ago passed from this world and the memories of people of this day.

That desire to actually soldier in combat has pushed a lot of us into situations we had no business being in. It put us in the wrong place at the wrong time, in the exact spot where hell was unleashed. Some of you know what I'm talking about; others might be moderately curious. I first wanted to fight a main battle tank, so for my first five years of army service, the place I lived in and called home was a mighty M-60A1 tank. It has a deadly 105-mm cannon, 50 calibre and 7.62-mm machine guns, and I eventually commanded one of these monsters. Later, when my dreams of flying finally came true, and I at-

tended and graduated from the US Army's rotary wing flight school in Alabama wearing a shiny set of silver wings, I knew I would fight as a pilot. I
would follow in my family's footsteps of carrying my nation's flag into battle
as an aviator.

Flying in West Germany (as it was then), I learned, practised and honed my
skills as a pilot flying the smallest aircraft we had, the OH-58 Kiowa Scout. It
may have been small, but its size gave it stealth, which could be used as a combat power multiplier by keeping track of the enemy's movements from afar. I
could be 'deadly' with a simple radio call; I could direct artillery fire or call in
an A-10 air strike. Flying in Germany made me rely on my instincts and I
learnt to push the envelope of my comfort zone. The weather is often bad
there and our aircraft were VFR (visual flight rules) only, meaning we could
not safely fly into clouds. We did it anyway, but back then, not many commanders were keeping score – unlike our current crop of micro-managing
military aviators.

That experience all paid off one day when a guy showed up from Fort
Campbell, Kentucky. Our meeting would change my life and it set me on a
collision course with that eventful day that would teach me what it was like
to be really scared while flying. He wanted me to interview for a classified
unit; hmmm…

"So what do you do?" I asked.

"Sorry, I can't discuss that!"

"OK then, what will I be flying, OH-58s?"

"No, we don't have any of those."

"Well then, what will I be doing?"

"You'll be a pilot – if you make it through training."

"So you're asking me to interview for a job I know nothing about, in some
kind of aircraft I'm not qualified in, and I might not make it anyway. Is that
what you're saying?"

"Essentially, yes, you have it right."

"OK, I'll do it."

That was it – in only a few minutes I had made a decision as momentous as
the 'I do' one. I had committed myself to a total change in my life without
realising it. It totally escaped me that no another aviator in the entire unit had
been asked to interview. Perhaps he thought I was the only one silly enough
to fall for a crazy deal like that.

Sometime later, things started to happen. Orders showed up that first took me to Fort Campbell and then to Fort Rucker for some advanced training. Soon afterwards, I got a phone call from a gentleman who identified himself as 'Sky King'. He asked me, "So, Mr. Harward, would you like to fly Blackhawks or Chinooks?" As it happened, I was looking out through the skylight in my third-storey German apartment at a Chinook flying overhead in the traffic pattern, apparently doing some training. I think I said something like, "Well, since the OH-58 is the smallest aircraft and the Chinook is the largest..." and before I could finish, just like that, this Sky King guy said, "OK then, Chinooks."

Boom! Just like that, I became a 'hook' driver. What Sky King hadn't waited to hear was the rest of my sentence, which was to have been, "Well, since the OH-58 is the smallest aircraft, and the Chinook is the largest, *I'll choose the one in the middle and take the Blackhawk*". Fate has a way with things like that. I think that to somehow make it all work out as it should, a higher power ensures some people hear what they want while others say just the wrong thing. I don't always understand it; I just live it.

Standing there with a dead phone in my hand – Sky King had hung up – I fixed my gaze upon that lone Chinook in the traffic pattern. It was carrying a sling load on its centre cargo hook; two 500-gallon rubber fuel blivets. As I watched it turn from downwind to base, the load suddenly released. The two blivets fell about 500 feet into a farmer's field and burst, spraying fuel everywhere. I could hardly believe my eyes. Less than twenty seconds ago, I had been told I was going to fly Chinooks and I was witnessing one have an accident. Was that fate messing with me again?

I can't tell you the unit I was assigned to because if I did, I'd have to kill you! What I can say is that for someone hoping to find himself in a fight, it was the place to be.

And so I became a Chinook pilot. As I had in Germany, I practised, honed my flying and perfected my skills – that would eventually be put to the test. One day, when we were out in the western US doing some training, I got a late night phone call. The voice on the phone told us to stop what we were doing, load up in the aircraft and get back to Campbell as quickly as possible. We did, taking off at around 0350 in the morning using NVGs. We flew all day and finished back on goggles arriving into Campbell Army Airfield. It had taken us over thirteen hours and my butt was dragging. I went into ops to see what was going on; the place was a buzz of activity. When I was told to standby for a briefing, I went to call my wife to tell her I was coming home soon. All the phones had their pig-tailed chords missing – someone had taken them. This was before the age of cell phones, so I was stuck.

The old man (commander) showed up and didn't mince his words. "Gentlemen," he said, "the president has ordered the invasion of Panama and we are to be the first in. Those of you who are fresh will fly the aircraft to Florida, refuel then fly straight to Panama. Those of you who just flew in, get on the C-5; you'll be leaving in about ten hours." There it was – no bones about it. By this time tomorrow, we would be at war and I'd be centre stage. I remembered the old saying: 'Be careful what you ask for – you just might get it.'

Several of the pilots, myself included, jumped on the giant Air Force C-5A Galaxy and rode backwards all the way to Panama, landing there around 2200. We were welcomed and told to rest as we were crewed first up in the morning. No ceremony, just work now.

When morning came, we 'hot-seated' a Chinook and immediately departed on a priority medevac mission. Flying out over the water and swinging in over the beach, we landed at the airport without incident. As we were preparing to load casualties, we got a change of mission.

As we were ready for take-off, CCT (centralised traffic control) – the tactical version of ATC – told us to watch out for a heavy weapon just over the fence. Being special ops, of course, we weren't too worried. We took off and started to accelerate, clearing the fence by a couple of feet. Perhaps thirty seconds later, I looked down and saw a jeep with a .50 cal machine gun firing right at us. We were so close to it that I could literally feel the concussive pressure of the weapon's firing. I just tightened up and grunted, and eventually we passed right over it. We got out alive, but only by the skin of our teeth; and so I was quickly inducted into the world of war. [*This attack is relayed in more detail in Chapter 6 – Ed.*]

That short 'war' taught me that tracers look like fireflies zipping past the windshield as they just sort of 'float around' briefly before ripping by at half a million miles an hour.

Do I still want to test myself? Unequivocally, NO! I don't need to do that again but I'm fairly certain I will. Although it will not be 'testing' next time, just surviving – and maybe even tipping the hand in our favour to 'win one for the Gipper'.

When I look at the young pilots strapping in their Apaches, Blackhawks, and Lynxes etc in the desert battlefields today, some still have that particular look of naivety that precedes their brush with a testing fate. Then there are the others – those who look more like us in the grey-haired crowd. Their eyes and ours convey something else – a certain knowing, mental control and a healthy respect for a twelfth-century people with simple small-arms weapons and the courage to use them.

I am careful and guarded in writing this closing paragraph. It is not a personal challenge from me, only an acknowledgement of that spirit that lives in the hearts of some of us. So, if you must, go forth, young warrior, and meet your match on a distant battlefield far away. As it says in Proverbs 27:17: "As iron sharpens iron, so one man sharpens another."

Like a siren song, the warrior spirit calls you.

"Come to this place and show me your best, for I wish to test you, to find your metal and see if it is strong and whether your heart is true. Show me your courage that you might really learn who you are. You are not like the thousands around you; you hear the distant thunder. Either your blood or that of your enemy will be spilt here, and perhaps only one of you will leave this place. Neither will leave as you came for I will change you forever."

Chapter 3

ON LEAVE AND
RETURNING TO DUTY

Going home on leave from a combat zone is always good – but always bad too. You sit in the airport knowing that at the other end of this flight, there will be smiling children and a loving wife, and days and days of stress-free freedom. But at the same time, in the middle of these thoughts is a feeling of impending doom that comes from knowing you will be coming back to this place – back to living from day to day thinking of and longing for home.

The flight home is always short, even though my last one was fifteen hours; nothing matters when I am on the way home. "Ladies and gentlemen, this is your captain speaking. We have just lost one of our wings, so you may experience some roughness for the next couple of minutes." No worries, I would think in my 'going home' frame of mind. We still have one good wing left – and didn't an F-15 recently land with one wing almost completely torn off? I'd subconsciously calculate the increased drag from all the ripped open wing surfaces and optimistically decide that it would be compensated for by the fact that the engine wasn't hanging there anymore. At worst, the flight might take a couple of extra hours as a result of the drag and missing engine. No, nothing bothers me once I'm on that freedom bird.

The flight home is just a 'space' between leaving here and being back on home soil and seeing their faces once more. As I step from the plane onto home soil, I often pause for a moment to burn the scene into my memory and consciously pull a chest full of American air. I wonder if business travellers ever feel the same when arriving home from a trip; I suspect not. However, I would-n't know; I've always been a returning warrior when coming home after a long tour.

As I stand there in the customs line, I wonder if I have earned the right to be here. Have I done enough? Do I really deserve all this – a clean airport, no fear of being shot or kidnapped? I don't need to check for exits or peer into the shadows looking for snipers. The bags all around me are just bags, not possible IEDs (improvised explosive devices), and people are just ordinary people, not possible gunmen. Whenever I'm away, I think of that break with my wife and kids as the highest award anyone could ever receive, and I wonder if I am I doing enough to deserve such an esteemed honour.

When the moment finally comes that I stand outside on the ground level at Cincinnati Airport, I don't care if it's freezing and I'm in a short-sleeved shirt. I just stand there looking toward the direction from which she will come. Then, like a miracle, it happens. I see that familiar Chevrolet Suburban approaching. At a distance, the glare on the windshield hides the faces of those inside but as it draws closer, out of the glare, I see her blonde hair. She's smiling widely and beside her is one of the girls, also smiling. Does any man deserve such a moment? I mentally record everything in my deepest memory banks to be recalled later, on another day, when I'm back here in this hostile desert.

As the car pulls up and stops, I stand for a long moment looking – first at her, then at the girls and the boys – my children. Then I swing the doors wide, and hug and kiss each of them. This is a moment that I treasure the most – a prayer answered; I am finally home.

According to my wife, my visits home comprise three distinct stages. Stage one is the honeymoon stage, during which all is right with the world. "Sure honey, you can have a new car and one-carat earrings; is there anything else you want?" The 'coming home' euphoria and the reunion are still having their ef-fects. It isn't real life yet, we're all just so happy to be together again.

My wife calls stage two the 'Holy crap – what happened?' stage. It is when I begin to think that the boys are misbehaving. Of course they aren't, but in my view, they are not perfectly disciplined little soldiers and have to be cor-rected. During this period, the little guys go and hide a lot. This stage is not an altogether pleasant time. But as with all things in life, it passes. I can tell when phase two begins to pass and phase three begins. One morning, I'll be sitting at the breakfast table with the boys and one will spill his milk on the floor. When he looks at me as if he has just committed a capital offence, I suddenly start to see him as a vulnerable little boy who is just a boy. This is the beginning of phase three.

Phase three happens for two distinct reasons. Number one is because we, as a family, have mostly worked through the emotional rollercoaster of our reunion after our long separation. And, of course, our separations are never 'ordinary', because inevitably my wife will have heard about helicopters being shot down in Afghanistan and had to deal with the sickening feelings of dread. However, I think the second reason is the most prevalent. It's a time when my wife and I realise that our time together will end shortly and we will be separated once again. Suddenly the small stuff no longer seems to matter very much. This is a time marked by a lot of hugging, a lot of listening and a lot of staring at loved ones. It is a time when we try to make the most of each moment – literally every moment. It is the time when I start snapping pictures of everyone and everything by the dozens…well, hundreds!

Phase three is a time of clinging to my loved ones. They know I am going to leave and that our time together is short. I know that not only do I have to leave them, but I also have to go back 'there'. Somehow I have to pull it out and be the 'man'. In my heart of hearts, I know what I am going back to. Once again, I'll have to deal with the uncertainty, the loneliness, the slow passage of time and the thoughts of what might happen to me. I love and hate phase three. I love it because I don't waste any time, and every moment counts. Life becomes amplified and I take what is mine, my God-given right to be happy and to enjoy. When I start to get down, I just think, "Well, at least I have today. I won't think about tomorrow; I'll just concentrate on what today has to offer."

Inevitably, the last day finally arrives. When I wake and roll out of bed, I'll stand there and look at my wife. Sometimes she's asleep; sometimes she peers at me through sleepy half-closed eyelids. I remember every single time that I have stood like that beside that English oak-framed bed and I remember how she looked. When I look at the mattress and realise it was my last night in that bed, I struggle with it; I never want to leave. Leaving is hard – much harder than most things I have to do in a combat zone. I don't want to leave my wife, my family, my home, my friends or my country. But like so many other soldiers, I can always hear the dim roar of the distant guns. A voice summons me towards the sound and I cannot run away from it.

During this time, I am a man torn between two worlds – my comfortable home and the world of war. Why am I drawn to it so strongly? Why is it so over-powering that I can hear those guns, even while others back home chat about day-to-day things? Maybe it's just a subconscious psychological ploy to give me the strength I need to come back to this dusty, hot place.

Time is so utterly relentless. Nothing can stop this single most irresistible force we face in life. It will continue no matter what we do.

Although everyone in our family tries to dismiss what is about to happen, the last day of leave is never pleasant and we all struggle with bouts of anger, fear, crying and nervous laughter. My wife will start the day by cooking breakfast before beginning a rushed, busy, cleaning frenzy. I used to wonder why she had to clean everything, sometimes twice. But if I were to stop her and force her to look at me, she would start crying and pull away before wiping away her tears and continuing to clean vigorously.

The last time that it was the final day, I remember her cleaning in the kitchen as I quietly packed; it was four o'clock and we were to leave for the airport at six. As she wiped off the stove and her eyes fell on the clock, she let out a long moan and just collapsed. She began crying and wouldn't stop; it was a bad day and I had to get my oldest daughter to drive me to the airport. Watching them drive away that day was one of the hardest things I have ever had to do in my entire life. Perhaps that was the most difficult day of leaving so far and it was five long months before I saw them once again.

Usually, when the appointed time comes, we silently load up in the Suburban. My wife usually drives while I sit in the right front; there is little conversation. The boys will chat about this or that while I note the passing of the familiar landmarks as we get ever closer to the airport. For my wife, this is the time when she begins to 'switch gears and tune me out' because she knows she has to become the strong one again, however much she might be twisted up inside. She knows the same thing I know, so we don't talk about it. All too soon, we drive up to the place where they will drop me off. Everyone gets out except for my youngest boys. One by one, I kiss them and hug them, and say goodbye.

I save my goodbye to my wife for last. We try to keep it together, but we never can. It is very, very tough, so I try to make it brief. In that last moment, I take in a lifetime of memories before she gets back in the car and drives off. I stand there and watch until the Chevy has disappeared completely, then I swallow hard, turn and walk away. We both know that it may well be the last time we ever see each other. I don't think business travellers have to go through that, but combat guys do and it is a damned hard thing to do.

Once, a long time ago, during Desert Storm, it suddenly occurred to me that I was a pilot in command of a helicopter in a special operations unit. Somehow this realisation had escaped me during the five months of build up and training in the Saudi desert. I suddenly realised just how much at risk I really was. You see, before that time, I only thought about how dangerous it was for the enemy. It never occurred to me that I could get killed too. I didn't imagine that they had any chance at all against us – it was going to be a one-sided deal, and we were going to pulverise them! Well, when the realisation did hit me, it must have showed. My commander noticed something was up and asked what was bothering me. I told him and asked him what he thought about it.

That commander, Major Russ Carmody, was one the finest men I have ever had the pleasure of knowing. A magnificent aviator, he loved to laugh and toss down a few from time to time, and we loved him. As an army warrant officer, he flew Cobras in Vietnam (his father was an admiral in the navy and was, coincidentally, also in Vietnam during Russ's tour of duty). I looked up to Major Carmody, not only as a hand-picked commander in a unit of hand-picked aviators but also as an iconic mentor.

> "You have to play a game to prepare yourself, Don", he said. "You have to make it right in your own mind. I used to think to myself how I'd lived a pretty good life – lived, loved, laughed and cried. I'd had friends and fights. I'd lost a few and won a few, and thought that if this was to be my day then so be it, because what I'd had was enough. My country and the army had been good to me, had spent a lot of money training me, and now I was one of the few soldiers who could do this mission, and it was my time to repay that debt."

His words struck a chord within me. "You know, sir, you're right. I have also lived a good life and if today *is* the day, then so be it!" That has been my silent thought and battle cry ever since. Russ Carmody and other men like him have unknowingly moulded me into the man I am today. For better or for worse, they have left their indelible marks. Russ couldn't win his final battle with cancer, but he fought to the end and was still serving as a lieutenant colonel in special forces when he passed. On the day he lost that last battle, America lost a fine man and a fearless warrior. Perhaps I owe him my very life – but that story is for another time.

In the lingering shadow of Russ Carmody and many other fine soldiers like him who have now gone, those of us who remain behind must carry the guidon of freedom and justice, and of things that are right and good. One has to feel this in one's heart to be able to go back because it takes something pretty meaningful to leave a wife and family, a home and a country – to put all these things behind you and get on that plane which will carry you off to a place of danger. I feel I must go back to earn my right to all these things I cherish. Money isn't enough, nor is the 'adventure' – not after having been at war many times. My father served honourably in World War II, so now it is my turn; I have to serve honourably so that my family name will remain unblemished. I have to earn the right to be called an American.

Chapter 4

MY LOVE/HATE RELATIONSHIP
WITH THE SLING-WING

The helicopter is a thing of beauty that just shouldn't work. After all, it's made of more moving parts than a dozen Swiss watches and assembled in such a way that the failure of even the smallest part would result in the total destruction of the whole machine. Its millions of ill-fitting and poorly adapted parts are purchased from hundreds of suppliers in dozens of countries and are finally assembled by the lowest bidder. It only flies because it shakes and vibrates so violently that the earth's surface actually repels it. The 'up' lever (named the 'collective') controls the amount of shaking, thus providing the amount of repulsive force which causes the earth to push it away — don't believe all that aerodynamics mumbo-jumbo, — which has not been proven. The thing turns right or left by somehow shaking more strongly on one side than the other. Thus causing the earth push-away effect to be stronger on one side — provided the whole congregation of parts somehow manages to stay more or less in one piece for an hour or two at a time in order to allow us to collect flight time and go from place to place.

Yesterday, as I was flying along in my naturally-nervous state (the result of my learned understanding of the machine, more of which later), I made the unholy mistake of touching something in the cockpit while in flight. (It was just a little plastic 'doo-da' that covers another plastic or metal 'doo-da'.) I touched it out of curiosity and then…bang – it suddenly broke. No Mr. Engineer, I didn't hit it; I just touched it!

I think I can technically explain why this happened. Inherent in helicopters of certain breeds is a nasty little effect known as ground resonance (which is proof of my theory of why the thing flies in the first place). These rotary-winged paint shakers can actually vibrate at a frequency that matches and reflects the ground they sit on. The result of this harmonic vibration can, and on occasion does, literally shake the whirly-bird to pieces. I'm not kidding. So, yesterday, I discovered that the effect could also manifest itself between my fingers and the helicopter. I must obviously vibrate at a frequency that my Huey doesn't like, so that if I touch a part at the wrong moment, it simply disintegrates.

Now, about the understanding I have with these machines: I know they are all death traps and that they have more creative ways of killing people than the writers' guild in Hollywood. I also know they are very moody and that they like to toy with pilots from time to time. They are not mechanical contrivances; perhaps they start that way, but they soon learn differently and start to develop moody behaviour. I am sure of this because when I'm lucky enough to be at home, I live in a house with four women. Helicopters act a lot like women, so I have learned not to apply reason or logic when flying them, but just sort of go with the flow. I look carefully at a helicopter during a pre-flight, not for missing or loose parts, which even a blind man can detect at forty paces. No, I look for what it's trying to tell me. Does it have that 'feel' like it may want to fly, or not? There are a certain few days when there's just no telling what it might do next, when reason and physics are thrown to the winds in total abandon.

I stand near it at first to see if I can pick up on this 'feeling' so that I'll know if it's safe to take it into the air. Sometimes I read it completely wrong. I was wrong more often in my earlier years, hence the numerous medals I wear on my uniform. I think that after several decades of flying these things, my average for predicting the mood of a helicopter is probably approaching fifty percent. This makes me something akin to a Yoda of the helicopter world. If I get the feeling that it, pardon me…she, would rather just sit the day out, then I find a reason to cancel the flight. I can always pull the weather card, "Yes, well, the mountain wave has produced a Coriolis effect, creating late afternoon dust devils and lower level disturbances." Or something like that.

Upon hearing this, civilian customers usually look around at the clear skies and twenty-five-mile visibility and say, "It looks pretty good to me, but you're the pilot, so if you say it's unsafe, well, I guess it's unsafe." Hah! Saved their lives and mine once again, and foiled the aluminium monster's plot to give me a bad day. In the end, if I cancel, it all works out fine. I get to surf the Internet, the customers get to live another day, and the bird gets a day off to sort itself out.

Please don't misunderstand me; I don't dislike the particular helicopters I'm flying now, or any others. No, I am actually quite fond of them in spite of all that I have learned about them. I just know that today is one day in the contraption's life that is in no way related to any other day in its life, but I still love them. Did I say love? I suppose that was a Freudian slip, and the truth's truth.

Then there are those days when you walk up to her and she is sitting there as pretty as a spring flower in a bed of snow. You can feel her (yes, helicopters are all female; although I have no idea where the males are or how they procreate) beckoning you toward her. When you flip on the battery switch to check the fuel level, the gauge springs to life with a certain urgent vigour and if it's in the evening, you will notice a soft glow of lights from the instrument panel. Hey, I'm not trying to sound kinky here; I'm just stating a fact. During the pre-flight, everything looks right. The hydraulic servos have all, sort of, settled in just the right spot and the bright chromed parts seem to be just a little brighter. After a pre-flight like that, I'll be willing to go flying in an approaching snow storm with a half-mile visibility.

I can tell even more when I start the engine and bring the thing to life. As the blades begin to spin, the various pumps don't make those terrible squealing sounds; they just smoothly start pumping vital fluids where they should go and not (as has happened in the past) all over me. Yeah, it is going to be a great day, all right. The N1 tachometer spools right up and settles into a smooth idle and, look at that, it's right in the perfect range. There's no doubt about it when she has been earthbound for too long and wants to push off and go flying. My final mental feel-good check is the moment when the blades suddenly and eagerly bite into the air as I start to raise the collective; the gear extends and then we're airborne.

I know the operator's manual says that on a given day, at a given temperature, weight, and altitude, it should take a prescribed amount of power to hover; but not on this day. Today she is spirited and eager. Like a thoroughbred racehorse, she feels as if she has become a fully compressed high tensile coil spring bursting with energy waiting to be released. Glancing down at the torque meter, I notice that she needs slightly less power to hover than the charts have predicted. I remember hearing that all life forces are in sync with one another through nature, or something like that. Make no mistake; a helicopter IS a life force, at least in the book of Don. If the earth senses that the mood is good, then it will give a little extra push just to say: "Have a good flight."

Such are the flights I remember while sipping iced tea (sweetened, thank you) on a sunny summer afternoon under the shade of a tall oak tree. I have had many such flights on many continents and I am a lucky man. My willing aircraft have shown me things that few others have seen or will ever see. So many things, that to talk about all of them would take a whole lifetime. I love and cherish so many memories of flying. I remember flying above a cotton-covered landscape near Würzburg, Germany, just as the sun rose into a bronze-gold sky, lacing it with streaks of red. And vivid in my mind is the image of cresting a mountain ridge here in Asia by fifty feet – only to find myself two miles above the ground just a couple seconds later. I could go on and on, but it would take more space than any editor would allow so I'll assume you get the picture.

There have been other days when things have been very different – when the aircraft has had sudden and unexplained mood changes while in flight. Yesterday was just such a day. Had I thought the helicopter was going to have a bad day, I would never have taken off but would have come up with a creative excuse about why we couldn't fly. However, I was subtly tricked into going flying and was already airborne when the sudden mood change occurred. Without notice, she suddenly decided to partially disintegrate. I know it was just one small part, but it was a signal. Feeling as if I was entering a minefield wearing snowshoes, I realised my next couple of steps could make all the difference. I wonder why I understand this so effectively with my aircraft but not with my wife.

I looked at the tiny shattered plastic part and pondered. There didn't seem to be any accompanying increase in the already-heavy vibration. The engine seemed to be normal, and the transmission was doing whatever it does in approximately the same manner as it had been. None of the crewmembers were reporting any smoke, fire, leaks or cracks developing in the machine, so perhaps the little shattered plastic part was just a warning. As luck would have it, a few minutes later, we made the inbound radio call to the firebase, which was our destination, and surprisingly, they refused to allow us to land. It seems they were busy shooting at enemy forces and wanted us to stay clear. It's always something!

Taking this as a definite sign, I immediately decided to turn around and return to base, because I knew she was getting cranky. As luck, or her mood would have it, we made it back without further incident and she flew smoothly all the way back. No fires, no emergency landings, no more parts falling off; only a slight covering of grease from the rotor system and we were safely down.

Two days ago, it was not so for another crew who took a bird into the wild blue without heeding the subtle warnings. Apparently, they had not felt the 'tremor in the force'. Less than two hours into their flight, they experienced their first transmission over-torque. Obviously, they had misread the signs and gone flying anyway; their bird did exactly what I would have imagined and rendered herself unflyable. Unfortunately, the crew did not learn their lesson. They should have walked away with their tails between their legs but instead, they decided to try it again. Their subsequent experience taught me that helicopters must actually communicate with one another. Bird number one was pissed off, and must have told their second aircraft, because by the time the crew returned to base with the second ship, it too was over-torqued. I know the earth must have been vibrating in the proper manner because the other aircraft in the flight logged eight hours without incident, so it must have been their particular aircraft's mood.

I know all helicopters are female. I now know they talk to each other. They obviously live together in the same hangar and flight line. Through my own experience, I know they all seem to have that bad week around the same time. If you haven't heard about this phenomenon, then sooner or later, you will. Before, when I flew airliners, it was easy; I'd simply bid for a five-day trip during that week so that I'd never have to experience the psycho ups and downs occurring at home. I'd also have the added bonus of flying in a much less moody, sleek looking, high-altitude airliner.

Here's the part I don't get: for the life of me, I just can't understand why helicopters are not consistent or predictable – they are all over the calendar and never seem to line up for any length of time. Contrarily, they'll just have a bad week once every so often for no good reason. Now why is that?

I concede that I do not know all that there is to know about helicopters – or women – though I probably do know more about the former than the latter; both are deep and enduring mysteries to me. Perhaps it is simply my place to sit back and enjoy the ride while being ever cautious of approaching doom. In many ways, I can identify with the main character in the 1959 movie Ben-Hur. There is a scene in that epic film where Hur is in a gladiatorial chariot being pulled by several magnificent white stallions at break-neck speed – never more than an inch or two away from doom. Well, that's me – I just hang on or strap in with little expectation for good or bad, and just smile in anticipation of the ride...

Chapter 5

RED SKY IN THE MORNING,
SAILORS TAKE WARNING

The convoy was moving along briskly, which was quite a surprise since convoys normally move like pond water. It was cold – and I mean, really cold. The free temperature gauge read zero, although I couldn't really see it. I was on 'nods' – our slang term for night vision goggles – and I was so cold that I didn't want to move my head at all. The doors in the back were open and the unfortunate gunners were literally hanging out in the freezing breeze. There was a good-humoured conversation going on in the helicopter, which I had started by saying, "Man, this sucks!" Jason, one of the two awesome warriors manning the guns in the back, replied, "I only wish it sucked a little more…and I'll bet Pete wishes it was raining too." Jason and Pete are both ex-marines – if there is such a thing.

Pete chipped in that rain actually wouldn't be such a bad idea after all because it would soon form a thick coating of ice, and he figured a coating of ice would at least make a good wind breaker. "Boy, I really wish I was a nugget back in the corps getting yelled at by the sergeant; yeah, that is where I'd like to be right now." However, when he added something about how the army (me) couldn't handle the cold without whining, I immediately put the aircraft out of trim on his side until we all could hear the wind noise coming from his mic. "Very funny!" he said. We flew on in silence for a while, freezing, until eventually, someone else piped up: "You know, this sucks…"

Bob was scanning his sector outside and occasionally glancing in at the dimly lit instruments. We keep the light low since the soft green glow on one's face makes a pretty good aiming point for a skilled sniper. We were flying at various altitudes looking for towers and fresh piles of rocks that could conceal IEDs or ambush sites. I watched the green circles of light from the goggle tubes lighting his face; he was all business and doing a good job. I wanted to transfer the controls to him so I could reach down to the heater vent to warm my fingers, but my time wasn't up just yet. We were flying thirty minutes on, thirty minutes off, and I had around ten more minutes to go.

Then I remembered that the heater wasn't working anyway. Earlier, when we took off at around 0500 we had tried everything including voodoo curses to get the *%^#!! thing to work…without success. The other day – when it was around sixty-five degrees Fahrenheit – it had worked just fine. Go figure. Now that we actually needed it, it wouldn't work. The thing had obviously been corrupted by the helicopter's black mood. I speculated that the heater control valve was probably frozen solid in a block of ice.

I moved my head just slightly…big mistake. My schmach (combat morphed scarf-looking thing) had been wrapped tightly around my neck and tucked into the back of my HGU-56 helmet. My slight movement had dislodged the fragile tuck of the schmach and opened up a hole through which icy cold air was now rushing and circulating around my head. You just can't leave well enough alone, can you, I thought, as I glanced down at the clock – there were still nine more minutes to go before I could say something manly like, "Well, that wasn't too bad," and be done with flying for another thirty minutes.

I realised that I hadn't felt my knees for quite some time, so I moved my legs or, more to the point, tried to move them. That awful numb feeling, followed by the tingle of blood starting to flow once again, reminded me of my total lack of planning while dressing earlier. In my defence, it was only 0330 when my alarm went off. I managed a shower and a shave, of around sixty percent of my face, at least, but missed the rest. While dressing, I forgot all about my long thermal underwear and left this vital layer of insulating clothing still folded nicely in my wall locker.

During our 0430 briefing, I think I still must have been in and out of REM sleep for at least half of it. I wasn't the only one who was 'feeling the pain' that morning. While sitting there, I noted Scotty was wearing his sunglasses and sat slumped slightly forward, while others were staring into their coffee mugs. Someone had talked about the weather, and the mission, or something along those lines, but now, it was all just a blur and as we approached a US firebase, I was thinking about, or rather, dreaming about, a warm cup of joe.

I looked down at the fuel gauge, which showed we still had around 1,000 lbs of fuel left. Over the past couple of years, I have developed a reputation for never getting too low on fuel. It isn't totally deserved, but nevertheless, I seem to have it. Perhaps it stems from the time when I flew Chinooks and we always had an extra ton or two of fuel on board. In any event, now, whenever I see numbers less than 5,000 on a gas gauge, it always makes me nervous. Then it hit me.

I suggested we refuel now, "so that my aircraft would be nicely staggered relative to the other aircraft". The air mission commander bought, I mean, liked, the idea, so we swooped in to refuel. Once we were on the ground, I thumbed Pete a twenty and sent him away for a warm brew while we filled our tanks. When Pete returned with four steaming mugs of joe and some egg burritos, life was suddenly good once again.

It was still Bob's thirty minutes, so he flew while I sat back and enjoyed my hot coffee. Bob would get his coffee, of course, but in about thirteen more minutes. It might even still be slightly warm by then…but probably not.

As we headed north, we flew into an increasingly colder and stronger wind. Our route took us past 'ambush alley' where the skeletons of burned out vehicles sat amid black smudge marks where they had been hit by RPGs (rocket-propelled grenades), run over mines or been blown into oblivion by IEDs. We gave the place a wide berth while Pete kept his weapon at the ready; he had been forced to use it in that spot earlier in the year.

We soon located the convoy and carefully scouted the area around and in front of it before Bob selected a gentle sandy knoll to land on. We had taken our goggles off just before we refuelled and the morning sun had now risen above the broken and rocky horizon. "Red skies…" Hmmm, what was that old saying? Jason said, "Red sky in the morning, sailors take warning; red sky at night, sailors' delight." I should have listened, but that morning hadn't started for me at 0800, so I flat out missed it.

While sitting on that knoll, the clock ticked away until it was my turn to take the controls once again and Bob could finally get started on his coffee; it was cold… I smiled. As the tail end of the convoy drove past about a half mile in front of us, I rolled up the throttle, recited the before take-off checklist and pulled the up lever. She (there's that word again) sprang off the ground. Didn't get light, wiggle or anything else; she just jumped eagerly into the air. That head wind must be increasing – it's taking less and less power to fly, I thought, and made a mental note of the fact.

We did the route reconnaissance and scouted ahead of the convoy – it all looked good. There was no enemy action, probably because everything around was frozen. I selected my next 'perch' to sit and run out my time. I ended up picking a wide-open expanse of flat desert. There was a wadi to the left that we could see up and down for at least half a mile. There were no villages nearby and the road was clearly visible for a few miles, so I would see the convoy approaching from our right.

I lowered the collective and pitched the nose up to start the approach. The lord of complacency must have been hard at work. I had a nice spot to land on, a good headwind and no reason for alarm. I eased in the power as we descended, trying to make it as smooth as possible, and Bob called the torque reading every few seconds. My desire to make the descent as smooth as possible was not to demonstrate my amazing skill, but simply because I was frozen and didn't want to move very much. It was a beautiful approach; I imagined guys on the ground sitting at a judging table and holding up score cards: five point nine, six point zero, five point nine, five point nine…

As the airspeed reached zero, we were descending through two feet. Through the developing dust cloud, I noted a smallish mound of dirt around fifty feet in front of me and to my right. Bob kept calling the torque reading: eighty-eight, ninety, ninety-two…Then, for no particular reason at all, the nose started an uncommanded yaw to the right.

What the hell? "Ninety-six, ninety-seven," said Bob – a reminder that the torque was almost maxed at 100 as I added a little left pedal to counter the spin. I didn't want to over-torque the machine so I said, "I'm going to just follow it around" – hoping it would just spin into the wind and stop. The dust cloud was really starting to build so I switched to looking out of the chin bubble for ground reference. Everything was OK until Pete said, "We're descending". Well, that was it. Up to that point, I had been trying to keep the torque below that magical 100 percent figure. However, now that was no longer a consideration. Were we to hit the ground while spinning, the probable consequence would be a nasty little thing helicopter pilots know as 'dynamic rollover' – which is exactly what it sounds like and is accompanied by a violent and rapid 'disassembly' of much of the helicopter. Unlike the computer game Halo 2, the helicopter does not then re-constitute itself moments later.

So I pulled up on the collective and although we continued to spin, at least we stayed above the ground. I wasn't about to reduce power or roll off the throttle, not with the increasing spin rate. In the next instant, someone called, "Rising terrain." We had spun a full ninety degrees and I was trying to fly out of it with forward cyclic. I realised we must be approaching that mound of dirt inside our thick cloud of billowing dust. No longer concerned about torque readings, I pulled in even more power. In about a slow two count, we emerged from the cloud of blowing dirt and as quickly as it had started, it was over.

As we began climbing at a good rate, the world below quickly got smaller, and I reduced power and levelled off at about 1,000 feet. I looked down and noticed the torque gauge was flashing – hmmm…not good. The flashing indicated an exceedance and the end of my nice frozen little day's flying. Bob ran through the checks and the telltale gauge displayed an unforgiving 104 percent. Damn! This was the first time I'd over-torqued an aircraft since an evasive manoeuvre I'd pulled on a particularly bad night during Desert Storm, and that one hadn't worked out particularly well.

So I did what any aviator would do: I tucked my tail between my legs, ate my slice of humble pie and flew back to the firebase where we had refuelled. Normally, after an over-torque like that, we might have considered landing immediately and let the maintenance guys do their thing in the field. However, had we done that, we would probably have appeared soon afterwards on Al Jazeera television wearing orange jump suits surrounded by guys wearing hoods and impatiently fingering rusty saws.

Happily, we had all walked away from the situation and tomorrow would be another day with its own new challenges. Such is the life of an aviator over here in this crazy world. That night after all the questions, debriefings, and speculation, I climbed into my bunk, pulled the green mink blanket up over my shoulders, took a long look at the picture of my wife and children, turned off the light and drifted off to sleep. Life seldom turns out the way any of us imagine it and, in the end, are we really in control at all?

Chapter 6

LUCKY
DOLLAR

Sometimes, we do things that make us wonder why we ever did them in the first place. Sometimes, we keep doing them for a long time — maybe even a lifetime. One such thing is the way I've been tucking the same old folded dollar in my wallet just behind my FAA pilot licence for many years. I know you can't see it, but trust me, it's there. I first put it there at around 0600 hours Central Standard Time, on 17 December 1989. Why is my memory of that time so precise, you ask? Read on...

It had been snowing and was as cold as the dickens when our giant C-5 took off from Fort Campbell, Kentucky. It was very different when we were greeted by a blast of hot tropical air on our arrival at Howard Air Force Base in the Republic of Panama at around 2300; what a difference from just a few hours earlier.

In the belly of our C-5 were two disassembled MH-47 Chinooks, all sorts of maintenance stuff and a couple of Chevy trucks along with about seventy soldiers. As the nose ramp lowered and settled on the tarmac, which was hopping busy with all sorts of activity, John, our group aviation life support equipment guy, walked up the ramp and shook my hand.

"Don, good to see you…better get some sleep; you're first up in the morning. 'H-hour' is set for 0045."

"Whoa, John; hold on there, big buddy. What 'H-hour'?"

"You didn't get the word en-route? The invasion is on and the thing goes down in an hour and forty-five minutes!"

His words settled in my thoughts as my eyes strayed from his face and over the surreal scene around us. All over the bustling ramp, crews were loading ammo, programming black boxes, pre-flighting and doing a hundred other things. Guys were lying on the ground, on the top of Blackhawk helicopters and all over the grass. I remember how the six-barrelled mini guns looked, silhouetted by the harsh floodlights positioned all over the ramp; 'potential energy', I thought. In just two hours, those silent guns would be glowing red from firing many thousands of 7.62-mm rounds.

"Yo, Don; grab your bags and follow me. We'll find you a cot." Like a robot, I did so and soon found myself inside a sprawling hangar with around 1,600 other special operations-types. I found a cot and claimed my few square feet of Panamanian paradise before going outside to help.

Crews made their final preparations amid the noise of APUs running, and main engines of Chinooks, Blackhawks and MH-6 'Little Birds' starting up. One by one, the various flights departed, variously laden with weapons, troops, gas and everything else imaginable, including the kitchen sink.

I stood outside the darkened hangar as H-hour approached. At exactly 0045, as I looked towards the Panamanian military headquarters, I heard two rockets smash into the building. Suddenly, one by one, everything opened up in a splendid light show. The neatest and most recognisable sound was the AC-130's six-barrelled, 20-mm Vulcan. The AC-130 was hammering everything with its Vulcan, 40-mm 'pom-pom' guns and deadly 105s.

It was quite unreal having a front row seat to the start of a war! After a few minutes, an officer came out and told us to get inside in case an over-zealous sniper appeared. I walked in and stood behind our S-2 (an intelligence officer), who was wearing a set of headphones. He was listening to the flight crews on the command frequencies as they got into the quickly developing battle. He was typing on the keyboard as fast as he could, and some other pilots and I read over his shoulder.

"Little Bird confirmed hit at grid…" was the first entry I noticed. Holy smokes, that was one of my friends, and we just took a hit. He paused and typed again: "Blackhawk confirmed hit in main transmission, making emergency landing, grid…" Within a minute, we'd lost a second one. Then almost immediately another entry: "Little bird confirmed shot down, grid…" No, way! This wasn't going well at all. Two minutes and two or possibly three aircraft hit already? The next entry was, "FARP (forward area refuel point; the place where, in a tactical setting, helicopters go to refuel and rearm) under fire; holding." The FARP was actually a Chinook helicopter full of gas, which had landed and was dispensing fuel to the combatants. Tomorrow morning was really only about four hours away; it was going to be busy.

At around 0600, my first mission, along with another Chinook, was to extract wounded army rangers from Tocumen International Airport. After a short flight, we landed near the smashed and broken main terminal building of the thoroughly blasted airport. Outside my cockpit, clearly visible through the chin bubble, was a corpse. In front of me was a Dodge Dart with four bodies hanging out, riddled with what looked like hundreds of bullet holes. Nearby, several prisoners stood zip-tied together awaiting transport.

While we were loading the injured, we got an urgent call for reinforcements over at Albrook Army Airfield; the PDF (Panama Defence Force) was making a play for the US base housing area there. I was wearing a kneeboard and writing on it like crazy, as I was not flying at the time. Every time I reached into my pocket, a pesky dollar bill kept falling out. I hastily folded it and stuck it under the clip on the kneeboard, I don't know why, but there it stayed. As quickly as we could, we then had to unload the injured and stuff our two Chinooks, and an air force MH-53J Pave Low, with as many rangers as we could fit.

As we took off, we told the air force tactical controllers that we were departing as a flight of three to the north. Although they advised us there was some kind of heavy weapon over there, for some reason, this did not seem to register. We pulled pitch and climbed out over the airfield fence, staying low and building speed. We were still accelerating when I saw it at twelve o'clock – a jeep-mounted fifty-calibre machine gun pointed right at my nose – or so it seemed. Everything was wrong; we were too slow, too low – maybe only fifty feet – and there was high ground to our right and left. Damn if he didn't have us dead to rights!

Out of ideas and with nowhere to go, we just pushed straight through it. To this day, I can't remember who was flying – but someone was. I just screamed a command: "Manny – fifty-cal just off the nose. Shoot him, shoot him." Manny, the left door gunner, who had the best angle, responded immediately at the same time as the fifty opened up on us. We were so close to it that the shaking of its muzzle blast thumped against my chest. I held my breath and waited for the rounds to tear us apart. I heard a single 'thump' from Manny's weapon and then nothing – no more firing from our own weapons, and the fifty went silent also. Manny's gun had jammed, but incredibly – by some unknown fortune – that fifty had somehow missed us.

Then I heard a second 'thump' and immediately smelled the burned powder. One of the rangers in the back had accidentally discharged his weapon inside the helicopter. We must have had forty or fifty guys in the back but, miraculously, the bullet hadn't hit any of them.

Then came the moment: I looked down at my kneeboard where I had been busy scratching notes, copying stuff and figuring fuel. In one of those 'Holy Crap' moments we sometimes have, my eyes focused on the dollar bill I had tucked under the clip. There it now sat in all its 'out-of-place' glory. I immediately recognised that folded dollar bill as my personal good luck charm. While the dollar bill didn't account for what had happened, at least it represented the events that had just taken place. As soon as that flight was over, I placed that dollar bill back into my wallet and have never flown so much as a kite without it!

If you think the story is over, think again. Fast-forward a year and a few weeks to the early morning on 17 January 1991 – the opening hour of Desert Storm. I found myself in the jump seat of the darkened cockpit of an MH-47 – call sign 'Python Five-zero' – this time, racing north towards Iraq. We were moving into position to cover the strike on Tallil, a large Iraqi Air Force base. We were the CSAR aircraft and we were pre-positioning to pick up any US Air Force guys who might not fare so well over the target. I was riding with Russ, our standardisation pilot, and Dan, a younger pilot who just arrived in country. Russ and I were supposed to have been the mission crew, but Dan needed some night desert-flying experience, so we agreed to let him fly until we got into the target area.

A maintenance delay meant we had been late getting out of the chocks and by 0345, we were nowhere near where we needed to be. The strikes had barely begun when the radio went into overdrive. The news we were receiving on the Satcom (satellite communications set) wasn't good.

"Python Five-zero, this is Shadow, over."
"Shadow, Python Five-zero, go."
"Python, we have a MiG north of you heading south. We are vectoring F-14s to engage; standby, over."

That wasn't good news. All around us, the terrain looked like a pool table, with nowhere to hide. If the MiG was just north of us, my money said the pilot was probably pretty pissed off because his base had just been smoked by a bunch of our bombers. I didn't need to say anything to the crew because they had all heard the radio transmission, but I told them to keep their heads up, as we had a MiG headed our way.

A couple of uneasy minutes passed before the right gunner said: "Sir, I have a high performance aircraft passing right overhead." I glanced down at my kneeboard. There was my 'lucky' dollar bill, folded and tucked under the clip – just as it had been a year earlier. I said a short prayer just as the crewman said, "Sir, that jet is turning, looks like he is turning into us, sir…sirrr!"

His rising voice told me everything I needed to know. We were dead; that was the MiG and he had us, plain and simple. It was all going to end right there. The aft gunner picked him up an instant later and started yelling: "He's coming right up our tail pipe. Do some pilot s★★t!"

Just then, there was a bright flash and someone yelled, "Missile, missile, break right, break right, NOW!" Russ, an expert pilot, slammed the cyclic right. At the same time, there was a second bright flash as our aircraft discharged a bunch of flares. I don't know whether the crew or the automatic countermeasures equipment punched the flares; didn't know, didn't care – all I knew was that I got one more breath.

Then almost immediately there was another flash and a second missile launched toward us. Everyone was yelling, and I was leaning forwards from the jump seat punching out flares and watching the scene. My mind was in hyper-drive; it was as if I could see everything at the same time. When the second missile also missed, I began to think we just might live to fly another day, until I started thinking this guy was going to get us – no matter what.

We were running flat out when we saw yet another flash. This one was different, not nearly as bright, so I knew it had been fired from some distance. Russ was doing all he could, but I had an idea; I yelled, "Climb, climb. Aft stick, aft stick!" As Russ complied, I fired a series of flares.

"OK," I said, "take the power out, roll this thing over and dive…Now, NOW!" As he did, I fired another volley of flares at the top of the turn. My idea was to decoy the missile up the path of hot flares, then 'go cold' and turn and dive. I hoped it would work, but I had no idea.

Thankfully, while the manoeuvre was successful and the missile missed, what happened next was just as dangerous. I yelled for Russ to land. I thought the MiG was determined to kill us and we should get out of the aircraft. Our dive was too steep and although Russ tried to pull a rabbit out of the hat, we hit with a heavy 'whump'. The aircraft started to break up, shedding parts all over. We left sheet metal, landing gear, antennas, fuel, oil and all manner of other debris scattered all over that desert.

Thinking we were now about to die from the crash, I had what some de-scribe as 'the clear' – a moment when everything makes sense and one sees what is really happening. I yelled, again, "Climb! Get out of here!" Russ did as he was told, and, incredibly, that Chinook hauled itself back into the air – badly broken, but still flying. Boeing, if I've never said it before, I'll say it publicly now: your Chinook is one outstanding aircraft.

And what about that MiG? Apparently, there never had been one. Imagine my surprise when I heard that. What there had been was a US F-15 that made a diving identification pass over us. Unfortunately, it had attracted so much attention that ground forces had fired three missiles at him (or us). Not that it really matters who the missiles were aimed at — the F-15 bugged out and we were left to deal with those deadly little shoulder-fired killers all by ourselves.

As quickly as we had started to crash, it was over and we were once again airborne, albeit in an aircraft that was losing systems fast. The master caution panel was lighting up like a Christmas tree: utility hydraulics, right boost pump, generator #1, generator #2, AFCS, and on and on.

We started running emergency procedures and while it wasn't pretty, we saved both flight boost hydraulic systems, one generator and one advanced flight control system (AFCS). We were having to cross feed the right engine from the left side, but all the important moving parts were still moving, and all of us were still breathing. We flew a short distance to a hide site we had established earlier and made what some would call a 'landing'. This was pretty tricky, since three of our original four landing gear legs were missing, but Russ, who was still on the controls, did an OK job of it.

The forward rotor blades skipped off the tarmac as the rotors coasted to a stop and it finally became silent. For a long moment, no one moved and I thought about everything that had just happened. My stuff had been scattered all over the flight deck, but when I found my banged up aluminium kneeboard, that folded dollar was still right there where I had left it.

I have read of brave B-17 crews flying missions over Nazi Germany wearing paper clips or rubber bands or girl's scarves or whatever. I wonder what puts notions in people's minds that there are such things as good luck charms; regardless, it doesn't really matter because they surely calm the thoughts sometimes. Maybe having a picture of the kids taped next to the altimeter or wearing a girlfriend's scarf instead of an issue item imparts some keenness of mind or eye — I don't pretend to know. I'm not going to question or debate it; there is just too much history there. You can call me old fashioned or superstitious if you like, but my quickly devaluing little dollar bill will stay in my wallet for many, many flights to come.

Chapter 7

COMBAT BOOTS
AND PICKLE SUITS

Combat boots is probably a familiar term to many, but what about pickle suits? It's a somewhat dated term, but I suppose I am somewhat dated also, which, I've come to appreciate, is not necessarily a bad thing. Pickle suit is the name given to the old one-piece green Nomex flight suit, which we all used to wear (and many still do). These days, pickle suits have become mostly tan or coyote-coloured flight suits festooned with a wide range of battle dress items.

For many years, I have worn such familiar one-piece flight suits as I've walked out the front door of my house, hotel, temporary housing and, on some occasions, the flaps of a tent. A flight suit is always comfortable and seemingly never out of style. It has set a style of its own that has even drifted into and out of mainstream fashion from time to time.

For me, the pickle suit is more than just clothing; it is my organiser. My pen is always there on my left upper sleeve; indeed, the one I'm wearing at the moment has a big black blob from the pen I left there the last time I washed the suit. My wallet always sits in the right lower leg pocket, my cell phone and comb goes in the left lower pocket, and important papers sit in the cool slanted zip pocket located just under the nametag.

When I am preparing for work, on top of my pickle suit, I wear a protective vest containing many layers of Kevlar cloth, which is designed to stop low-velocity bullets and bomb fragments. Inside a pocket, and outside the Kevlar on my front, is a 'class four' hard-armour plate, cleverly contoured to fit my body. This solid, heavy mass can stop not only a 7.62-mm bullet, but also the much nastier 5.56 bullet. The little 5.56-mm devil has a 62-grain bullet with a tungsten steel core that will drill a nasty little hole through most armour plate and render its wearer wondering why he or she just got shot. My plate stops both, even after multiple strikes. Outside the vest is the 'Mollie', which is a network of nylon webbing to which we attach various pouches. I carry two double M4 carbine thirty-round magazines, a first aid pouch, two tourniquets, two pistol magazine pouches, a grenade pouch, a radio pouch and another pouch crammed full of every imaginable extra, including my GPS and all-weather matches.

I carry a helmet bag and a runaway bag over my shoulder to and from my helicopter. The runaway bag is not some childhood hangover, but a smallish sack filled with extra ammunition, medical stuff, a change of socks and underwear, a space blanket, a built-in water bladder, some money and other things I might need in a jam. On my right upper thigh, I carry a pistol securely retained in a drop leg holster from which I can draw it quickly and snap off two shots in only a second or two. In my right hand, I carry a trusty Colt M4 carbine with a double thirty-round magazine locked into the magazine well. On the back of my head, I wear an old ball cap. Also desert tan in colour, my cap is a little dirty and slightly worn, and has a black and white flag sewn to its front. Around my neck, I wear my wife's scarf and sometimes I catch the scent of her perfume from it.

Even though my pickle suit and other essential battle dress or 'kit' are usually very familiar to me, one day, their appearance caught me totally by surprise. I was walking across the ramp away from my helicopter after a particularly hairy mission on a foreign border and was lost in thought about the preceding few hours. We had carried out one of those pre-dawn take-offs for a very early strike designed to catch the bad guys off guard.

It was still early morning and the sun was still coming up. As I walked, I was in one of those 'thousand-mile stares' when I happened to glance down at the ground. The angle of the sun caught me just right to cast a deep shadow. For a moment, I stopped and looked at the shadow. It was as if it were another person – the kind of person one might see in passing who catches one's eye and makes one stare. The shadow was bent forward under the considerable weight it was carrying, with lots of bulges and protrusions all over. Perpendicular to the upright shadow was the all too familiar silhouette of the M4 carbine the figure carried. With its well-known triangular front sight post and 'birdcage' flash hider, the weapon is simultaneously feared and loved the world over.

As I gazed upon this figure, it suddenly hit me − it was the silhouette of a soldier. I'd seen it a thousand times in the grunts, weary from several days of fighting, who I'd carried in the various helicopters I'd flown. I'd seen it in soldiers at home in the US, in Europe, Asia, Southwest Asia, and too many other countries to mention.

Then the second realisation hit me. It was me I was looking at; I was the soldier. As we navigate through this obstacle course called life, we sometimes forget who we really are. Then come moments of clarity when we see the naked truth and it all suddenly makes sense. So it was for me − there on the ground in that slightly bent-forward shape, I saw the real me − a soldier, still...

A few hours earlier, Steve and I had just taken off from the coalition base from which we were launching the assault. The LZ we had been to was situated at 10,000 feet − that's right, we made a combat assault landing at 10,000 feet − and we did it in a Huey! This was a feat in itself, but the worst part was that it was the only LZ in the area. Had anyone been lucky enough to clock one of us on that very narrow little landing spot, then the guys on the ground would have been on their own because there would have been no way for anyone else to come in and pull them out. It would have been a blood bath − splashed all over the world's media.

I remember looking behind me, as we flew, I could barely see Beano, the medic who was crewing our aircraft, scanning outside through the open right door. His M4, with a grenade launcher attached, moved about at his side in the wind. On the floor were four troops secured under two cargo straps. As well as having removed the doors, we had stripped out all the seats, dropped all our extra junk and even reduced our fuel to a mere 1,000 lbs. All of these measures were essential in order to give us enough of a power margin to land at that height with our weight.

In front of us, the formation was well spread out as we climbed. Normally, we would have been flying much lower, but the valley floor sat below at around 3,000 feet, while the LZ sat at 10,000 and the peaks soared well above that. Several ships were maintaining position in a formation called a 'combat spread', which gives an aircraft a general position, but allows room for quick manoeuvre should one or more aircraft be engaged by ground fire. There wasn't a lot of cockpit talk; it was pretty much all business, but the command radio frequency was alive with radio calls and code words. Each time I heard one, I would mark it off on the Execution Matrix that listed the code words, in sequence, of the various waypoints and mission tasks. I noted on the last call that there weren't too many entries remaining before the one marked 'Arrive LZ'.

So far, so good, as the several flights of assault aircraft drew ever closer to their destination. As we flew level at about 9,500 feet, the jagged mountains at our twelve o'clock were a menacing stark contrast to the smooth desert floor a mile and a half below us. The troops in the back looked at me every time I looked aft. For all we knew, these might have been the last few moments of our lives, but it didn't matter. This thing was in motion and nothing was going to stop it. I heard the code word for 'gunship overhead landing zone', which also meant that 'Chalk 1' from the lead flight would be in the flare to land. (We call aircraft in a formation 'Chalk'; the first is 'Chalk 1', the second is 'Chalk 2' and so on.)

This was the most likely time to run into trouble, but we heard Chalk 1 call clear of the LZ as Chalk 2 flared for his landing. Four ships were to land in the first flight before us; we were Chalk 2 of our flight. We were positioned two minutes in trail behind the lead flight. I was on the controls and it would be my approach and I knew I had to nail it. The overhead photos showed it to be really tiny, barely the size of our aircraft, but what the overhead photo didn't show was vertical features; it all seemed flat.

Another code word – the one designated for 'last aircraft clear'. I lifted my hand off the collective and looked in the back. I held up two fingers and yelled: "Two minutes!" I paused for a moment and looked into their eyes. I always do that because it makes it more personal for me. I do better knowing there are human beings in the back and that they are the reason I am here.

We approached the landing zone, which was ahead and to my right. We were flying on the right side of a very narrow box canyon in which the LZ was about 200 or 300 feet below the ridgeline on a small outcrop of rock. The solid rock wall to my right seemed impossibly close, and while I set up on approach, the winds were already buffeting us. There could be no excuses; this had to be perfect. I watched as lead flared and thumped down. He was on the ground for barely a second before I saw troops sliding out of the aircraft. The guys on the left side had to be careful not to fall right off the cliff to their deaths as there was a drop of 500 feet or so on that side of that LZ ten feet or so from the skid! I warned Beano (names have been changed to protect the innocent) about the drop. I couldn't see him anymore, as he was busy cutting the straps we used to secure the troops.

As lead pulled up and then dived down the slope in a hard left turn, I set my power and rode an imaginary glide slope down. I always imagine a string extending from the tip of my nose to the touchdown spot and I adjust power as necessary to stay right on it. At fifty feet above the ground, I started the flare. Sliding forward in my seat allowed me to see just over the nose as it rose to block my view in the deceleration. Steve was calling power: "fifty–five… sixty…sixty-five." Just as he said seventy, the aft skid touched down. I lowered the collective about half way, and the Huey rocked forward and slid, maybe, three feet.

Before we had even stopped, the shooters were getting off. I heard a "Let's go" from the back, and pulled in power. The 1,800 plus horsepower of the Lycoming 703 answered eagerly and we leapt off the ground. "Two's clear," Steve called on the radio. I cranked the cyclic left and reduced power. The rotors bit into the thin air and the aircraft came around quickly. We dived to gain airspeed down that steep slope – losing altitude like a brick covered with hot butter until a slight tug aft on the cyclic ended our rollercoaster ride and we rounded out several hundred feet above the valley below at about 120 knots.

"See anything…? We take any fire or hits?" I asked. I got a satisfying, "Don't think so; we're clean. Let's get out of here." Above me, Mike in the gunship was covering our departure. If anyone had fired on us, his team would have made minced meat out of them. Through the greenhouse (the tinted Plexiglas window above the pilot's head), I saw the gun bird pull up and turn away to cover the next ship's arrival. As always, Mike – a former Apache pilot, with a killer's instinct – was doing a great job. He was all over it on that mission and ready for a fight.

Before I took off that morning, I had prayed a simple prayer for protection, my head bowed and one hand on the dusty nose of my aircraft. As we cleared the LZ and headed for home, it seemed my prayer had been answered. Of the more than fifty reported enemy, either they hadn't been there, or they were unwilling to fight. They could have pressed an attack and destroyed one of our aircraft on the LZ and it could easily have been mine. But this day, there had been no fight. This day, peace had prevailed and we all got to go home one more time.

To a soldier flying a mission, it really doesn't matter if a fight is the final outcome. Exactly the same mental gymnastics are required before starting the approach. You have already prayed and you continue to do so. In your mind, it's all go, even if the 12.7-mm round blasts out your windshield, and you, on short final. You are prepared for anything to happen, and although you are more scared than most people will ever be, you press on anyway. Maybe that's why, in Vietnam, one army aviator after another persevered with their missions and continued to land, despite seeing other ships in their formations getting shot to pieces. In the end, a soldier just does what he or she was sent to do. The heart is racing, the adrenaline is flowing and one is overcome by a state of 'hyper–awareness' as if the world had slowed down. Bullets or not, bodies and minds still pay the price.

Such were my thoughts as I stared at my shadow that day. That silhouette had seen and felt the danger on many occasions in the past. Some days that shadow had bounced in happy elation over tough missions accomplished successfully; other days had not been so kind. But on this day, my soldier's shadow rested – motionless and thankful.

Chapter 8

OF A HALO
AND FATE

The helicopter we were looking for was white and huge – a giant Russian-built Mi-26 'Halo' – which had a cargo bay about the same size as that of a C130 Hercules. A couple of minutes ago, its pilot had called that he was five minutes out, so he should be in view. Jason saw him first, reporting on the intercom that he was almost overhead. I snapped my Huey into a bank to look upward and acquired the big aircraft almost instantly. We were orbiting just to the east of Tarin Kowt (TK) at about 1,000 feet AGL and had just cleared the pass we thought the Halo would fly through.

Russian pilots definitely do not think like western and, more specifically, American crews. We are very tactically minded and operate as though someone is always just about to blast us out of the sky. The Russians just climb up into the wild blue yonder and turn on the cruise control. Later, they make long slow descents when they finally get to where they are going. This crew had been cruising at 13,000 feet, well beyond small-arms range and probably out of sight for most potential threats, and that was OK with me. Today, my job was to get this big sucker safely to TK (which, at the time, was Taliban central) and safely home again.

The Russian captain flew to a point above TK airfield and started his painfully slow spiralling descent. I imagined the Taliban on the ground, who could surely see this monster approaching by now, would be calling all their buddies about the big fat juicy target descending into range of their weapons.

The gun bird I was flying was equipped with two menacing multi-barrelled machine guns manned by a couple guys who really knew how to use them. I wasn't worried about our safety; if anyone in our helicopter saw anyone shooting at us, we'd have them at the gates of paradise in less than ten seconds. However, I was concerned about those Russians and that big white helicopter.

Figuring that the most dangerous threat to them would possibly be a shoulder-fired, surface-to-air missile, I decided to climb up and tuck in behind them. We were equipped with devices that could conceivably defeat an unsophisticated missile, so I reasoned that if I tucked in close enough and someone toggled one at us, hopefully my decoy devices would protect both of us.

I moved into a position about three to four disk lengths away at a forty-five degree angle from its right side and slightly above the bigger machine. From here, if it were hit and exploded, it would still be unpleasant for us – but it would be far worse if we dipped into the rotor wash of that monster.

From then on, the flying was easy and gradual; I guess a fifty-ton helicopter doesn't do anything very quickly. Even as it turned onto final for the 6,000 foot dirt runway below, we were still far from safe.

Just the night before, a major fight had broken out between the Taliban and the 10th US Mountain Division right at the airfield's front gate; that fight had ended when a 500-lb GPS-guided bomb had found its mark.

Inside the thick, bullet-proof dirt-filled Hesco barriers next to the runway was the refuel point or FARP. Parked alongside the FARP was a bullet-riddled AH-64 Apache helicopter; it had collected all the bullet holes in exactly the same airspace we were currently flying through, so no, this job wasn't over by a long shot.

As the Halo dropped below 100 feet, his massive seven-bladed rotor system started to kick up a world-class dust cloud. It was time for me to bug out, which I did with a climbing right turn to cover his six; I was hoping we might catch someone aiming a machine gun at that big white bulls-eye, but we saw nothing.

The SAR bird, which was number two in our formation, had been covering me also, and we both continued in the turn and dropped into the FARP for a much needed sip of gas. To our right, a giant mile-long dust cloud that had been created by the Halo was drifting our way. "Great, just great, here comes a dirt shower," I said over the intercom. The gunners, who had begun refuelling the Huey, turned their heads and zipped their flight suits up as high as they could as they saw the wall of approaching dirt.

There was nothing we could do in the front; we had been flying without doors, and the dust and dirt immediately swirled through the cockpit. I glanced over at Dick and saw him holding his hand below his helmet visor to avoid eating too much dirt. I was holding the controls, so all I could do was to wait it out as the grit filled my mouth and eyes. Thankfully, it passed as quickly as it had begun, although it left a blanket of dust covering everything including the radio faces so that I could no longer see what frequency we were tuned to.

By now, the Halo had already taxied off the runway and on to a pad of PSP (pierced steel planking) panels. His rotors were stopped and the ramp was down. With an 'Up' call from Chalk-Two, I rolled the throttle up to flight and we re-positioned to a couple of small pads near the Halo. As we shut down, all manner of cargo was pouring out of the bowels of that monster, including a couple of F250 trucks, pallets, boxes, lengths of steel, pipe and plywood. It looked like they were setting up for market.

Curious, I walked the short distance over to the Halo for a closer look. Inside the hold, the loadmaster was busy coordinating the unloading of his aircraft. I went up front and climbed the ladder to the flight deck. The flight crew – captain, first officer, navigator and flight engineer – were all sitting around eating fruit. "Looks good," I said, breaking the ice as I leaned against a bulkhead near the door.

The navigator was the only English speaker, and he graciously offered me a smallish seat and some melon slices before he began to show me around the spacious cockpit. To me, it looked like something from the 1940s. The instruments were extra large and looked like they came from a steam locomotive. The flight performance computer was nothing more than a piece of paper under a glass panel, on which one could move mechanical horizontal and vertical lines. The navigation station looked like another cockpit display. I asked the young navigator what he used to navigate around the country. He smiled and tapped a Garmin GPS receiver, which was attached with Velcro to the top of his panel. I started laughing and the whole crew erupted in laughter right along with me.

I gestured with my hand. "I'm Don, what is your name?" The young man said: "I am Yuri." He then pointed to the engineer. "He is Yuri also." Next, he introduced the captain – also a Yuri. I couldn't help asking somewhat sceptically, "Another Yuri?" The captain listened to the navigator translating and laughed and said in rough, broken English: "Yes, I am Yuri also!" OK, great, three Yuris in the same cockpit. "And you, sir; what is your name?" I asked the first officer. I am not making this up, and, as far as I know, they were not kidding me, but, you guessed it, all four men in the four-man cockpit were named Yuri!

The captain moved aside and motioned for me to take his seat at the front, which I did. Sitting there, I gazed over the 'other team's' approach to rotary wing design. It definitely lacked the fit, finish and technology I had grown ac-customed to, but there was no denying what this beast could do as far as lifting massive loads. The Mi-26 is a rotary wing superstar; nothing else on earth can out-lift it.

We traded a couple of stories and they asked about me and what I used to do. Of course, in my professional past, I had trained very hard to make large numbers of men like these cease to exist – and now they were our 'friends'. The navigator mentioned that the captain once flew Mi-8 helicopters for the Russian military in Afghanistan. "You know, we Russians once fought here," he said. I smiled and looked the captain directly in the eyes and said, "Yes, I know. You fought against the Afghanis – and the Americans." You could have heard a pin drop after that one, but I held my stare as his face turned back into a smile and he said something in Russian that the red-faced young navigator did not trans-late. I guess that while all soldiers are probably the same in some ways and share much common ground, as far as politics go – at least from this old soldier's point of view – the thing between the US of A and the Russian bear is far from over.

Unfortunately for the Russian crew, English is the primary language of the coalition forces, and is used by air traffic control and others. With the navigator being their only English speaker, these guys hadn't adhered to a single clearance, and further, had not followed the route they had been briefed. Again, the differ-ence between the eastern and western minds was very apparent. We like to meticulously plan our routes based on weather, aircraft performance, the enemy situation, fuel and other factors. The Russians just blast off, head where they want, and get there whenever they want to. Essentially, we had exposed ourselves to danger for nothing by reconnoitring and clearing a route that the Russian crew had just ignored; I wanted to make darned sure that they followed the rules going back up north on the return flight. They didn't, of course, but that's an-other story.

The youngest Yuri took a moment to visit my Huey crew, and he sat in my seat and put my helmet on. We showed him a couple of things up the front and then took him back to show him the GAU-17 mini guns. Those things just look evil; all those barrels and feed chutes choked with cartridges. It was the business end of the Huey gunship and he was impressed.

As I walked with him back to the Halo, he showed me a photo of his wife and daughter. They lived outside Moscow in a nice part of town. He had grad-uated from a military school and, like everyone else, had been thrown into the civil commercial flying world without much of a clue. Although his pay was just a fraction of what western guys get, he was doing well. To me, he reflected new hope for his country. This smart young man loved his family and was willing to make sacrifices to give them a decent lifestyle.

Soon after this visit, the crew and their Halo moved to Kandahar and I began to see them regularly around the base and in the dining facility. They parked their white Behemoth not very far away from the Huey ramp, so – along with half of Kandahar airfield – we got to 'enjoy' regular dustings whenever it landed at its gravel pad.

One day, during the winter of the following year, there was a nasty snow-storm with low ceilings and reduced visibility. We had just cancelled a planned mission because we did not have the minimum visibility required to fly when I saw the Halo starting its engines. Because the weather was so bad, I assumed it must be some kind of maintenance run-up but the rotors spun up and the beast taxied out of its parking bay and onto the main taxiway.

While 'normal business' for the Russians is anything but normal, by now, I was watching with interest. To my surprise, and that of everyone else who was watching, that thing picked up to a hover. Then we realised it was not just a hover; the thing was still going up. Then, amazingly, the nose pitched forwards and away he went…that maniac just took off. I went inside to recheck the weather to see if I had misread something but, no, I had it right – one mile with moderate snow, 500 foot ceilings with icing conditions, mountains obscured.

That was probably around eight or nine in the morning. That evening, while we were eating supper in the mess hall, someone came in to find us (we were on standby) and told us that the Halo had made it into TK (its destina-tion), but had not been heard of since it departed there several hours earlier. I knew from having been there often that TK was only around forty minutes flight time away; it didn't look promising. We finished up and went straight back to operations. The news definitely wasn't good. Still no one had heard from the Halo and, best case, even if it had made an emergency landing because of the weather, the chances were that the Taliban would probably already have found the crew.

We were directed to prepare for a search mission under night vision goggles. We had been up all day, but everyone was still ready to go anyway. Unfortu-nately, there were moderate to severe icing conditions and visibility was still less than a mile in snow. After some consideration, it was decided we would launch at dawn and follow a direct course, which we assumed the Russians would have probably done, as they loved to use their GPS with only one point – the destination.

The news got much worse shortly thereafter when the Taliban announced that they had just shot down a large helicopter, and there were reports from locals of an explosion and fire. The army had sent a special forces (SF) team to the area to investigate and they were already in the vicinity of the reported explosion.

The following morning, we were briefed that the SF guys had indeed found what looked like parts of an aircraft scattered all over the side of an 8,000 foot mountain, although they couldn't get all the way up the mountain because of the weather. The Halo was the only aircraft missing; it appeared that it had not landed to avoid the weather.

Before we launched at first light, I thought of my conversation with Yuri about his family. I hoped that if anyone had survived the crash, maybe – just maybe – they'd also survived the freezing night.

The crash site was little more than a black smudge a couple of hundred feet below a jagged ridgeline. There was no sign of life. There had obviously been a fire and helicopter parts of all sizes were scattered all over the place. Knowing what I know of flying, I can say they were probably *not* shot down. What probably happened was simply CFIT, or controlled flight into terrain. If only they had climbed another 500 feet higher, they would have made it. Unfortunately, they found the highest point between Kandahar and TK, violently and suddenly.

Too many flying stories end like that. I heard a few from my Dad, others from old warriors – I've read a few, and I've lived a few myself. They all reinforce the importance of grabbing onto life with both hands and holding on with all one's strength, because for any us, there might just be a hard granite wall waiting inside a soft white cloud at some point when we least expect it.

I'm not going to dwell on it. I look at it like this: I woke up this morning and my name was not in the obituaries; it's a good day already!

Chapter 9

AIRMEN AND
SOLDIERS

I am always amazed by soldiers, seldom by politicians and almost never by celebrities. Here on the front, we get to see a lot of all of the above. The politicians are always buzzing about seeking answers, or maybe just wanting to get out from inside the beltway and 'hang out with the boys'. Some time ago, some senior Washington-types were staying in the spare rooms alongside mine. I wonder if they even noticed the fact that we didn't acknowledge them. You see, to us, the guys on the ground are the real men – like the two special forces commo guys who were all alone at a forward operating base for months without relief (the base is named after a heroic special forces soldier who died there). If aliens suddenly abducted those two remaining soldiers, there wouldn't be so much as a whisper on national news, but they continue to serve their country while forsaking their families and personal lives, day-in and day-out.

Over time, I have become immune to and do not notice the subtle change that takes place in me when flying in a hostile environment. As a result of spending all my time dealing with facts, without knowing it, my sensitivities seem to slowly disappear (just ask my wife). A while ago, I had to carry a gentleman from one nation's embassy to his base. Unfortunately, his headquarters lie in the middle of a city where the Taliban roams at will, routinely blowing up people and buildings. It was a dangerous place but I had been assigned to fly him there. My crew gave him the required safety briefing before the flight, much the same as a flight attendant would have on a normal domestic flight. Then it was my turn.

I told him we would be flying over the desert at around 500 feet and that when we neared the 'objective', I would descend to rooftop level and increase speed. I warned him to expect abrupt manoeuvring, but that this was normal. The poor guy stared at me with a 'what have I got myself into?' look.

Then I got serious:

> "If we go down in the desert, stay with the aircraft; it will probably be a controlled landing. The sat-phone is in my right pocket. Get it and pull yourself – and anybody else you find – out of the aircraft. However, if we go down in the city, we will be literally surrounded; I will try to land or crash next to a walled compound if I can. Grab my rifle, get out of the aircraft and get inside the compound and hold it until help arrives. If you stay outside, you will probably not survive, so get inside with as many of the crew as you can. If I'm not alive, take my vest; it has eight M4 carbine magazines and a radio and first aid kit. If any crew members are with you, follow their orders instantly; if not, then God speed."

I realised I had scared the hell out of him, but it didn't seem to matter all that much to me; am I losing my compassion? You see, there is a huge difference in perspective between his world and mine. I was simply telling him what he needed to know in order to survive and I wasn't interested in the delivery technique. (Note to self: when you get home, do not say a thing – let the wife and kids do all the talking.) Pity me if I ever have to go back to flying commercial airliners, imagine if I slip up while making the PA announcement.

That flight was one he will undoubtedly remember for a long time. Crossing the river, we 'jinked' sharply right then left until over the city. I selected a wide street and flew down it at about fifty feet while maintaining speed as long as possible. Approaching the compound, we flared steeply, dissipating airspeed quickly as we crossed the wall before descending the thirty or so feet into the relative safety of the landing pad 'inside the wire'.

While off-loading, I maintained power and stayed light on the skids in case a mortar round landed nearby. As soon as our passenger was clear, we took off, but not on a reciprocal heading, circled the compound in a tight orbit and accelerated. As we reached ninety knots, I rolled the helicopter out over another alley, which led to a graveyard and then the river. That way, if we had taken a round in the engine, there might have been a place to auto-rotate that was free of 'cumulo-concrete'.

It is one thing to get shot down, but quite another to get shot down *and* crash into a building; the sudden stoppage can ruin your day. In my mind, I always envision the rotor blades being neatly sheared off if we go down between buildings and the aircraft landing straight ahead with the dirty side down – but do I think that is how it would really happen? Fortunately, we were soon back across the river to the relative safety of the farmland.

On another occasion recently, I gave a similar briefing to another official visitor I had been tasked to fly. The difference that day was that we were flying in the gunship instead of the more 'civilised' CSAR aircraft. This meant she would be riding with the helicopter whose job it was to fight if necessary. I had to tell her that if a fight started, my job was to fly into it and place the bird in a steep orbit over the hostiles to allow our weapons to bear. We would not be able to run until those we were protecting were clear, but would purposely turn into the shooting and return fire. She didn't seem to have a problem with it and flew happily with us for hours.

I remember thinking one Sunday how bad I had it when, with the temperature in the 120-degree range and dust everywhere, I had to walk to church because there were no vehicles available. I walked in to the sanctuary of Fraise Chapel and took a seat. When we all stood to sing, I noticed a young man in the front row who did not stand. The fact was, he could not. I then noticed he had one of those portable metal stands with an IV bag and a plastic line standing beside him. He was in the front row and he sat there alone. When the chaplain, a young captain from the 10th Mountain Division, asked for prayer requests and praise reports, the soldier raised his arm, the one with the IV still in it.

"Chaplain, could we pray for the guys in my squad who are worse off than me? And, sir, for a praise report, I'm still alive and I'd like to thank God!"

The statement was simple, succinct and dead honest – much as soldiers' lives are. I later learned he had been the victim of an IED (improvised explosive device) and that this particular church visit was the first time he had been out of the hospital since he was wounded. I felt ashamed of myself for having felt hard done by, not having a vehicle and having to walk – at least I *could* walk.

I recently spent a little time in a hospital in Afghanistan and as I lay there quietly, what I saw was surreal to the point of disbelief. One night, there was a mass-cal; the abbreviated term used to describe the arrival of mass or multiple casualties. There had been a fight, which we had won – but had also lost. I watched as the wounded came in, one after the other. Multiple sorties by Black-hawk helicopters ferried casualties to the medevac pad just outside the building. There was screaming, barking of orders, some people were moaning in pain and some were slowly dying. The latter were quiet, mostly. The beds filled up quickly. The soldier beside me had no leg below the knee and was burned across his face and neck; in fact, he didn't appear to have much skin left at all. Directly across from me was another who was badly burned and was missing an eye.

Two surgical procedures were being carried out in the hallway because the operating room was already occupied. An Afghani soldier looked at me with his remaining uninjured eye as a Canadian surgeon spoke to him through an Afghani interpreter. The surgeon matter-of-factly told the interpreter to explain to the soldier that he had lost an eye and was about to be shipped out to another hospital in Bagram. As the interpreter translated the doctor's message, the Afghani soldier's remaining eye was fixed on me. Although his lips were trembling, he kept a straight face, not wanting to show weakness. However, I knew that he realised he was a ruined man and that his life was forever changed. His gaze held me captive – one man in great pain and distress reaching out to another; cultural differences lose their significance in a field hospital at a time like that. I prayed for him – I don't care what religion he observed; he was just a man in need of help.

When I use the term 'soldier', I really mean all those who carry heavy rucksacks and move about in worn 'leather personnel carriers' (boots), for it is they who shoulder the responsibility for protecting our mighty nation. They could be infantrymen, air force FACs (forward air controllers), sailors, marines or special forces 'soldiers'. At heart, they are really the same; although to ask them, you would think each is uniquely better than the rest. I see that as a healthy thing. Many have been the times that one or another of the various warrior communities has given me grief over my use of the term 'soldier'.

If you are unsure of the military background of the person you are speaking to, simply call him a soldier. A marine will instantly correct you. Just yesterday, as we sat parked at a firebase waiting to make a second sortie, I was lying resting under the belly of our helicopter and talking to Jimmy (one of the gunners on my aircraft and a former marine). When I called him a soldier, he immediately responded by asking me, "Do you know what the word 'army' means? Ain't Ready for the Marines Yet." Funny! A sailor? Well, you can just tell, and there's no mistaking an air force person's techno-acronym babble. Former army personnel will just nod in the affirmative and continue to listen.

For wounded soldiers, the outcomes and stories are not always bad. Just because life in general, or a powerful explosive in particular, might have changed their lives, they still manage to maintain their strength of spirit and care for each other. Once you have been a soldier, particularly if you have been blooded, you are forever part of a brotherhood that transcends your personal life.

Last summer, it was almost a nightly event for our camp to be struck by rockets (typically Iranian-supplied), which usually came in pairs. After such explosions, most of us would walk outside to look around; combat gawkers! It is some-times funny when new people arrive here. If you are quick enough to get outside right after an attack, you can watch them scurrying around, running into the nearest bomb shelters, or tripping and falling. The seasoned veterans simply climb on top of something to see if they can get an idea where the rockets landed. One night, as I lay in my bed, the camp was rocked by a couple of powerful ex-plosions and I figured we had been hit by a couple of 107-mm rockets. Most of the time, these impacted somewhere innocuous and exploded harmlessly – punching holes in taxiways or hitting open fields. It was not the case this night. As I looked towards the 'boardwalk' (a place where soldiers congregate around the post's Burger King), I saw flashing lights. I heard someone in our group say that we had unaccounted-for personnel. I jumped into our Humvee (army Hummer) and drove down there. The streets were blocked off and there were lots of ambulances on the scene.

This time, the rocket had hit our dining facility during the evening meal. I felt helpless and could do no more than send an email to my church back home, asking the good citizens there to start praying for those who had been wounded. The prayer worked, there were no fatalities; the surgeons (saints) saved them and the wounded were evacuated to Germany for treatment in Landstuhl Regional Medical Center, the Walter Reed of Europe.

It wasn't long after this that I was hospitalised in Afghanistan and was also shipped out to Landstuhl for treatment, where I ended up in the same ward as some of the casualties from the rocket attack. One afternoon, I was chatting with one of those gentlemen, an army major who had been really torn up. However, he had a cheerful spirit and a good sense of humour. "You know," he said, "all I did was go to get a bite to eat and… BOOM! Now I have a second a★★★hole! The shrapnel entered right here," pointing to his posterior. "I'm all done now. Career is over; I guess I'm going home." I asked him what he did for the army. He replied, "I'm a lawyer," then added, "I guess I'm now twice the a★★★hole that I used to be!" I laughed harder than I had in a long, long time. Can you be-lieve that man's personal courage?

There is no doubt that aircraft are critically important to modern warfare. Sometimes, the only way to get around or be re-supplied is by aircraft. Here in Afghanistan, the bad guys are not doing all that well against aircraft. They are usually on the receiving end, and the sound of an Apache or an F-16 might be the last thing they ever hear. Therefore, it has become important to them to shoot down aircraft for much-needed psychological victories. Shoot down one of our helicopters, and CNN will amplify Al Jazeera's story and provide all the free press that the Taliban or al-Qaeda can handle. This probably makes flying a little more dangerous for our flight crews, but I doubt we will get a break from the media anytime soon.

We aviators get a lot of the press because we fly very expensive machines – generally on missions of high visibility or critical importance, which means we usually get recognised if something goes really wrong. Remember Mogadishu, Somalia? That mission went wrong when a young ranger fell from the fast rope and 'Blackhawk Down' happened. While the pilots on that mission do deserve a lot of credit, it was really the guys on the ground that deserved the recognition. Much of the respect given to pilots is really not deserved because after the helicopter or airplane flies away, the grunt still remains. Nevertheless, it sometimes still happens to be that way.

There may well be some who think of my writing as rambling. I care not. These are my thoughts and my feelings; they come from my heart and they guide my pen. When I think about soldiers being wounded – or worse – it always gets me into a knot. I feel deeply for them, because I know I can never match their heroic and selfless sacrifices. They are truly the real 'Great Americans' in my book. God bless them all.

Chapter 10

WHAT IS A 'NORMAL' LIFE?

You know, sometimes, life can be normal – even when it isn't. Let me explain. While getting ready for a mission one morning, I was in the shower trying to rinse off the sleep just like millions of people do every day all across the world. While trying to figure out which bottle was the shampoo and which one was the soap, a simple task which fifty-two years of showering experience has not made easier, I heard what I thought was Scotty banging into the thin wall that separated his room from mine. I thought he must have rolled over in his sleep and bashed his arm or his head on the wall; he's a big boy.

Then about five seconds later, the building shook. Hmmm – not Scotty sleeping violently after all. Now, I realised it was the shock from a rocket shell exploding somewhere close by. This had been rocket number one, and they almost always come in pairs. I glanced out of the smallish window in my shower to the parking lot. There, I saw Pete – a large-framed ex-South African special forces medic – standing in the back of our F250 pick-up truck. He was looking towards the runway and the revetments where the army parked some of its helicopters. This was an area that the Taliban gunners had 'zeroed in' on (as much as it is possible to 'zero in' an unguided rocket) during the previous summer.

However those Taliban gunners had themselves been 'zeroed in' upon last summer and had long since departed this planet for paradise, so we had pretty much all but forgotten about the frequent attacks on our aircraft. Thankfully, the latest Taliban rocketeers appeared to have inherited the aiming skills of their deceased predecessors. They got a little lucky, but not really; there was a little damage to one aircraft but nothing more.

One of our weapons mechanics had been walking back from the mess hall at the time and was pretty close to the impact. He had been strolling along when he heard the whizzing sound of the inbound rocket. He commented that it got a lot louder pretty quickly, so he hit the dirt. It was a good thing, as shrapnel landed all around him when it exploded.

As I was towelling off after my shower, the phone rang; it was my lovely wife. We chatted about the normal stuff. "How's your day going dear?" "Well, we've just had a rocket attack. The battles are still going on in the Helmand, and I forgot to make the Visa payment." "Oh, OK. Well, I'm tired and it's late. I was just missing you, so have a good day. Love you. Bye." See what I mean? This was completely 'normal' to me. It's strange how we adapt to all sorts of situations.

GUNFIGHTS AND HELICOPTERS

A couple of weeks later, I was enjoying a day off, and it started off great. I had slept in until being woken by the sound of our aircraft taking off on a support mission at around 0800. I got out of bed, suited up for my morning run and departed. Later, as I was cooling down and thinking of the warm cup of coffee that awaited me, I strolled past operations on the way back to my room. I heard a lot of radio traffic coming from the building, so I stuck my head in. Jeff, who was on duty, and Jack were listening to the high frequency radio; I asked them what was up. Jeff, an ex-special forces aviator who gets calm when he's serious, said, calmly: "The ground guys have been hit and our guys are currently engaged."

Man, it always comes just like that. One minute you're thinking about drinking a cup of coffee; the next microsecond you're switching gears and getting your game face on. "How bad?" I asked. Jeff replied that two of our aircraft had been hit.

Knowing what was surely coming, I walked straight to our remaining helicopter and pre-flighted it in about five minutes. Then I headed back to my room, put on my flight suit and returned to operations where I listened to the radio traffic; we were getting hammered! This was shaping up to be a very bad day. Jeff and Jack both told me to stand by to launch.

It is not normally allowed, and is not tactically sound, to launch a single aircraft. With no mutual support, you stand little chance if you're unfortunate enough to get shot down. So to launch that bird would be considered a high-risk mission. The military evaluates each mission according to many different and complicated criteria, and assesses it as low-, medium- or high-risk. Low- and medium-risk missions may be approved locally, but to launch a high-risk mission required the permission of the ambassador or his designated representative.

That process was moving forward and we felt certain we were going to launch – it was just a matter of time. Outside, the mechanics were busy preparing our aircraft as a gunship. It was not a normal gunship configuration, but had a multi-barrelled mini gun on the right side and a (single-barrelled) M240 machine gun on the left. Because we only had one gunner instead of the usual two, he would have to strap in with a 'pig tail' harness and move from side to side as necessary.

Listening to the radio was surreal. I heard Dennis say: "Taking heavy, and I mean heavy, good fire from the tree line." Then Fox 29 ('Foxtrot 29', the ground element commander) called that he had casualties and requested medevac. That meant our CSAR bird would have to land in the middle of all that mess. While Fox 29 was transmitting, we could hear the sounds of bullets smashing into his truck.

And then all hell started to break loose. The tide of the battle definitely began shifting to the Taliban. They shot two more of our people and quickly destroyed several of our vehicles. Panic started to set in amongst the Afghan forces on the ground. They tried to drive across a river to get out of the 'kill zone'. As they did, the vehicles began sinking in the mud and were getting hit, forcing their occupants to swim for their lives – under fire! Meanwhile, the convoy that was trying to get out of the battle area ran into an ambush from three sides. They took a casualty right away and got pinned down.

There was only one gunship on the mission and it was pretty busy. It was getting shot again and again, and I realised we might soon be looking at another 'Mogadishu'. I felt it wouldn't be long before we had birds shot down, and whenever that happens, the battle always goes into overdrive. I'm sure there is some psychological reason why enemy forces think it is 'better' to shoot down an aircraft than to get a ground soldier or a vehicle but I can't understand why. I had seen it happen time and time again, and I could see it happening again. Jeff was trying to hasten the launch approval process because he could also see what was coming.

Dennis took fire again as he made another pass to try and identify the enemy who had mixed themselves in with the locals. The Taliban were wearing burqas (Muslim women's headdress) to disguise themselves, making things extremely difficult for Dennis's gunners to pick their targets.

Things were steadily getting worse. Mike and I were squirming in our seats in our desire to get there and help as we heard that fifteen to twenty heavily-armed men were crossing the river. Finally, we got the approval to launch and we were off the ground within ten minutes.

After taking off, we tuned in to the battle frequency and listened. Two of our birds were down at a nearby base with battle damage that rendered them unflyable. The only remaining bird was unarmed except for its crew's personal weapons. That left us as the only remaining gun bird available, and we were twenty minutes away.

As the guys on the ground escaped – abandoning their vehicles and heading for high ground – the Taliban allowed them to go; after all, they had won the day. By the time we were halfway there, the fighting had stopped and what was left of the convoy had driven out. The wounded were in the trauma hospital, thanks to our aircraft and medics, and we were licking our wounds.

Earlier in the fight, Fox 29 had called for the QRF (quick reaction force), which is a highly-mobile, combat-heavy force that can be quickly deployed for just such an occasion. The QRF in Tarin Kowt, where the fight took place, was Dutch. They are the force (and I shudder to use that word when referring to the Dutch) that the ISAF (International Security Assistance Force) had placed there.

The American philosophy in Afghanistan is to call on the Taliban to disarm and cease activities. When they refuse, we destroy them. This philosophy is simple, to the point and effective. And believe me, they understand it very well. However, the Dutch philosophy regarding the Taliban is to make them irrelevant. It might read well, like something one might hear in philosophy or political science class in college, but it simply doesn't work.

The Taliban take advantage of being 'irrelevant' to rearm, reequip, retrain and fortify. As a result, they had gained strength in the Tarin Kowt area again to the point where they actually placed checkpoints on the roads, and terrorised local farmers and merchants. It was unbelievable. The Taliban just loved this cosy arrangement with the Dutch and seldom harassed them. Therefore, activity around Tarin Kowt had decreased to the point where it appeared rather peaceful. If it were up to me, I'd send two brigades of the 101st Airborne in there for about two weeks – but that's just me.

The Dutch are not warriors. They never did manage to launch the '*quick*' reaction force to come to our aid. However, while we were flying toward the battle area as fast as we could, the Dutch eventually launched two Apache helicopters, which climbed to several thousand feet over the area. From this altitude, the only things they could see were our vehicles still stuck in the shallow river –which they promptly turned into beer can sized parts with a couple of Hellfire missiles. Good job, boys. (Note to Ford Motor Company: your trucks are no match for Hellfire missiles.)

Another memorable participant from that fight was John Sable, whom we had nicknamed 'New Guy', as he had only been in Afghanistan for a month or two by the time of this fight and was one of the newest pilots flying with us.

John was the AMC on that day, which made him the man in charge. He did well, considering his inexperience, and although his aircraft were getting hit and the guys on the ground were taking casualties, he maintained a cool head. He kept it all going and, at the end of the day, we had no fatalities, thanks, in part, to his decision-making abilities. (John later earned himself a second nickname, which is a rare treat indeed. Not long after his first fight, he was again the AMC on another mission. Just like the earlier occasion, he was providing convoy coverage, when, once again, the convoy got hit and people were shot. As a result of his apparent attraction for enemy fire and metal projectiles, 'New Guy' became known as 'Magnet Ass'.)

We were soon approaching the bowl in which Tarin Kowt sits from the south. We knew exactly where the fight had taken place, but as we came up through the last pass, it looked peaceful and strangely beautiful. As we flew over a wadi, I looked down and saw a man holding an AK-47 assault rifle, staring up at us as we passed overhead. I got the distinct feeling that he must have had enough for one day and there wasn't any fight left in him. There was no doubt that the Taliban would have taken some casualties when our gunners had returned fire, as there is simply nowhere to hide from those heinous mini guns.

With the battle over, we swung wide to the east to avoid the area completely. All three of our other aircraft were on the ground in the FOB (forward operating base) a couple of miles away. For us, there would be no fight, but that is just fine with me. I have no love for the fight and I had every intention of fulfilling my promise to my wife to come home safely.

As we reached the FOB, the damaged aircraft sat with their cowlings open while the crews inspected the battle damage. What I saw and photographed was unbelievable. The gunship had been hit numerous times. The main rotor system had one huge bullet hole right through one of its control rods, while another bullet had hit the rotor blade pitch horn and still another had penetrated one of the blades near the main spar. There was even a bullet entry hole in the roof of the helicopter, which says something about the bank angles the pilot must have been flying! The auxiliary fuel tank had been hit and the thick power cable to the right mini gun had been severed by a bullet. A bullet had passed through the armoured floor and through a roll of duct tape lying right next to the gunner, while another passed through a piece of the aircraft structure only a few inches from his head. The pilot's seat had been hit, as had the aircraft's nose. A bullet or piece of shrapnel had pierced the gunner's body armour, and some electrical wiring had been severed.

The CSAR bird had a single bullet pass through its tail boom. That same bullet then passed right through the tail rotor control tube, almost severing it completely. Thankfully, the machines stayed together long enough for their crews to get them on the ground in a safe area.

Just another 'normal' day.

Above left: Author, pointing, beside an OH–58A. Mitch Launius is at the controls. He and I were the two young (and dumb) pilots of chapter sixteen. We tried to test fly one of these aircraft without permission or qualification to do so. Giebelstadt, Germany, 1981.

Above: Desert Storm: King Khalid Military City (KKMC), Saudi Arabia, Jan 1991. B Company, 2nd Battalion 160 Special Operations Aviation Regiment. Author standing extreme left, Major Russ Carmody centre forward.

Left: Author in left seat of AW139 just at take-off.

Below: Author cruising along in N140EV, southern Afghanistan.

Top: The 'Stallion Ramp' at Kandahar airfield (KAF), August 2009.

Above left: Flying south of Kandahar airfield and north of the city.

Middle right: AW139 in flight in southern Afghanistan.

Above right: FOB (forward operating base) north west of Kandahar city. Many firefights have taken place in the vicinity of this base and a couple of helicopters have been shot down in the hills just to the north.

Above and left: AW139 on approach to FOB.

Bottom: Kandahar Lake, a man-made reservoir and the water supply for the city.

Top: The KAF Christmas 2007 group shot showing the aircrew that was on the ground for the holy day. Regardless of the holiday and the desire to be home, we were required to man the unit at sufficient strength to support emergency or contingency activities. Thankfully, and mostly due to the cold, the Taliban did not conduct a lot of insurgent activities in December.

Above: John 'New Guy' Sable (on left) and Scott Birdsell. Scotty is modelling Danish army desert outerwear!

Left: Gerry Ernst, pilot. Gerry was also serving as a US Air Force lieutenant colonel flying C130s when he wasn't spending time with us flying our Huey gunships and CSAR aircraft.

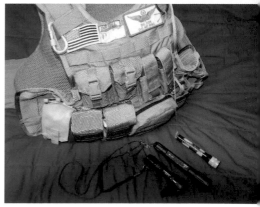

Top: Pilots on the ground, Christmas 2007, KAF. L-R, Bob Drury, Gerry 'Big Head' Ernst, Billy Walker, Don Harward, Scott 'Scotty' Birdsell, John 'New Guy' Sable.

Above left: SAR Medic Larry Reeves and author. Both formerly served in US Army special operations units. Larry was a 'Green Beret' medic.

Above right: Christmas in combat means getting a brand new vest. This one topped the scales at forty-five lbs.

Left: The dollar bill the author still carries with him, along with dirty nomex gloves and a wallet from his girls given at Christmas.

Top and Above: Mi-26 Halo arriving at Tarin Kowt or 'TK' as it is known. This is the very aircraft talked about in chapter eight.

Above: The Mi-26 is the world's largest and heaviest production helicopter. Not very manoeuvrable, it is nonetheless able to sling load a damaged US Army or British Chinook helicopter for transport off the battlefield and back to base for repair.

Left: Author in the captain's seat inside the Mi-26 Halo of chapter eight. By modern standards, this aircraft is dated, but one heck of a workhorse.

Below left: Author behind the Halo while it refuelled in Qalat.

Top: Burger King at KAF, 2006 located at an area known as 'the board walk'. This spot is frequented by US, Canadian, British, Dutch, and other ISAF soldiers for some relaxation. In 2010 a rocket exploded near this spot killing a soldier.

Middle left: French soldiers escorting the body of one of their fallen soldiers to the C160 that will carry the body home for burial. 'Kilo Ramp' KAF, 2006.

Middle right: Dick Edington, the lead pilot, guiding one of our aircraft into parking at Herat, 2006.

Above left and right: Fraise Chapel of chapter nine, on KAF, near the boardwalk.

Chapter 11

LITTLE BOYS AND
FLYING DREAMS

My earliest recollection of a chance meeting with the 'flying bug' happened when I was six or seven years old. My father had taken me to the Baltimore civic centre for some sort of a technology show and some father-son time. While we were wandering inside that spacious building, I gazed at the various displays of technological wonder. We turned a corner and there it was right in front of me – a Bell 47 helicopter with its large Plexiglas bubble staring outward like some enormous praying mantis. The rope placed all around it was meant to keep people away, but it did nothing to stop me. I was drawn like a moth to a flame and it pulled me ever closer.

My Dad had apparently lost track of my whereabouts, because he would have immediately called for me to come back out of the restricted area, or perhaps I couldn't hear any longer because this thing was beckoning me onward. I walked right up to the skid and climbed up into the cockpit. Without giving it any conscious thought, I plopped down into the seat and grabbed the cyclic. In my vivid imagination, I could see the white and yellow rotor blade spinning wildly and the world slipping below my feet. The pedals were too far away to reach but the cyclic was firmly in my grasp. As I pushed that stick forward, the flight controls made a squeaking sound, and, just like that, I was centre stage. Outside that protective plastic bubble, there seemed to be a thousand eyes staring at me. Dad hopped the rope and was on me in a flash. He smiled and pulled me out of the seat muttering apologies to the onlookers, a couple of whom were probably the owners.

Something happened to me at that moment; a seed was unknowingly planted during that innocent and chance encounter. I wouldn't know it for many years, but these machines would someday carry me across faraway lands and afford me special views of this planet which few have ever seen.

Years later, as I approached my teen years, I was again out with my father, only this time we were fishing at Atkinson reservoir, a lake created by the army corps of engineers back in the 1940s. It was a place that gave refuge to large-mouth bass, a favourite game fish that are a hoot to catch.

As my father and I worked our ancient spinner baits under a clear summer sky, all at once the thunder came. At first it was just a low rumble but it built quickly. Dad wasn't looking down at the water any longer but was staring toward the dam that impounded the lake. As the rumble quickly became a roar, I got scared. Then I saw it! Streaking across the lake like a bullet was an F-4 Phantom jet fighter, and that sucker was right on the deck. It ripped past the dam and filled the valley with such a cacophony of sound that it was felt rather than heard. I saw every detail of it – its camouflage paint, the angle of its wings and tail, and its twin turbojet engines. It blasted past us in a flash and then pulled up to clear the hill a mile or so distant.

As I watched it pass from left to right, Dad came into my field of view and I saw his eyes fixed on it also. He turned towards me as the fighter pulled abruptly upward, making a distinct ripping sound. I must have looked as if I had seen the second coming – awestruck is not a powerful enough word to describe how I felt. As the jet climbed skyward and the sound faded, I refocused on my father's eyes, which were now fixed on mine. With just a hint of a smile, he asked me, "Don, would you like to fly one of those?" The weight of that question was amazing. I was just a boy and flying that Phantom was several thousand miles beyond anything I could imagine just then. I simply answered: "No Dad, I could never do that." Turning to look toward the now distant thunder he told me: "Yes you can, if you really want to." If that wasn't another seed, then it was certainly a healthy helping of fertiliser for my earlier dreams of flying someday.

Many years later, I had a son of my own; I was eventually blessed with three sons but at this time, only number one had arrived. I had named him Don after my father and me, and since everyone always seemed to call me 'Big Don', he naturally became 'Little Don'. The army had posted me to Germany, where my unit made its home at Kitzingen Army Airfield. One chilly late autumn Sunday, Little Don and I had driven into the hangar so I could wash the car inside where there was some precious heat. Just outside the hangar on the apron was a helicopter refuel point. While I busied myself vacuuming and scrubbing the car, one aircraft after another taxied into the refuel area for a sip of jet gas. I had opened the heavy doors of the hangar a few inches to allow 'Little D' to get a look at the aircraft while still keeping him safely inside.

As I ran my chamois cloth along the contours of my Pontiac Trans Am, I heard the snarl and growl of an AH-1 Cobra attack helicopter hovering into position to refuel. Finishing the aft quarter panel of the car, I glanced over to check on 'Little Don', only to discover that he wasn't where he had been just a moment or two before. I glanced quickly around the crowded hangar looking for him. In one of those moments of clear understanding, I shot a look back towards the hangar door where he had been. As I heard the engine of the Cobra rolling back up to flight, I immediately knew where that boy had gone. Like an Olympic sprinter, I dashed towards the opening in the door. I couldn't get through it fast enough and one glance toward the snake (slang term for the deadly Cobra) confirmed my fears.

Dividing the street from the flight operations area where the refuel pits were was a five or six foot tall anchor fence. My son was on the helicopter side of it, perhaps only thirty feet away from the running helicopter. I pushed with all my strength and started to part the heavy hangar doors far enough for me to get through. My near-panic began to evaporate as I saw Little Don pinned back against the fence by the full force of the rotor wash from the five-ton Cobra. Despite the noise and windblast, he was still waving his arms wildly and trying to jump up and down. As the Snake came to a three-foot hover, instead of turning towards the runway, it made a ninety degree turn to face my son, nose-to-nose. The nose-mounted cannon, usually kept in a barrel-up position, dipped momentarily in greeting then slewed upward as the ship turned left and took off from the pad. As I ran to reach my son, I remembered the little boy who watched in awe as the F-4 streaked by at treetop level.

Just as my father had done all those years ago, I, too, studied my son's eyes and when he finally looked at me, I asked, "Son, would you like to fly that some day?" Although he did not answer, I saw a change take place right there in front of me. A spark had ignited a small flame and, thanks to my Dad before me, I recognised that event for what it was.

Fast forward ten or twelve years. Now a slightly greying master army aviator, I thought it was time to have the career choices talk with my now teenage son. Sometimes I smile when I realise how everything is carefully orchestrated, but we blind humans still believe in chance or coincidence. By the mid-nineties, my army career was getting a little long in the tooth, and Little Don, who wasn't so little any more, was approaching the end of his high school years and thinking about what might lie beyond. I always saw a spark in his eyes when we talked about anything to do with flying. Indeed, aviation had become so much a part of his life through me, that the two were becoming indistinguishable. I felt in my heart of hearts that my son needed to take his place amongst other aviators who would forsake their own lives, if necessary, to defend our great country.

It was a summer evening when I decided to talk to him about his career choices. Sitting in the living room as usual after supper, I asked Don what he wanted to do with the rest of his life. "You know, Dad, I'm just not sure yet." As fate, or perhaps a slightly higher authority, would have it, just at that moment, the sound of a Blackhawk helicopter began to drone its steady beat. We lived directly south of Fort Campbell, Kentucky where nearly 500 helicopters reside and one of these was apparently going out for some night training.

Don twisted in his seat on the couch and moved the curtain aside to try to get a glimpse of the approaching Sikorsky. Seeing this, I pressed, "So what is it that you have a passion for; what do you dream of doing?" Again, he said he didn't know, as he moved the curtain from side to side, straining to see the helicopter. As the sound of the rotors grew ever louder, I asked, "You don't feel passionate about anything – nothing comes to mind?" The Hawk was flying at about 300 feet and was going to pass right over the house.

Don couldn't stand it any longer and rushed outside to stand on the front lawn. I hurried out after him and we both looked up as that cargo hook passed right over our heads at a few hundred feet. I watched Don look after the Blackhawk as it passed from view behind a big southern pine tree. He turned and spoke, "Dad, I just don't know!" Sometimes you just can't decide if you should laugh or cry or hit them on the head with a big stick!

Little Don did eventually serve his country as a flying enlisted soldier in the Air National Guard, where he flew as an aeroscout observer in OH-58 Kiowas.

With some people I have known, that spark of passion could not be suppressed. The best such example I can think of was Jody Egnor. A man of average stature and fairly unremarkable in appearance, he was anything but 'average' or 'unremarkable' in the dark cockpit of an army helicopter, where he excelled. I often thought of him like a son and my memories of him are as strong as ever.

I first met Jody when I reported to my final unit of assignment in the US Army. When I arrived, the company was deployed to the field on a major training exercise and I thought I'd get a couple of weeks relaxation in the 'rear area' while awaiting their return. My hopes were dashed when word came back to have me report immediately to the field site. Reluctantly, I loaded my newly issued gear into a Hummer and was driven out to a muddy, nasty spot on the map called 'Golden Hawk'. Who comes up with these names, anyway?

The Hummer stopped on a piece of terra firma – which wasn't – and we threw my bags out onto some less muddy weeds. As the Hummer drove off, I was standing there wondering where everyone was, when young Warrant Officer Jody Egnor approached me with a big Midwestern smile and shook my hand. "You must be Big Don. You're expected; let me get your bags." Jody would have probably carried all of them had I not intervened. I followed him into the tree line and the large tent that was to be my home for the next couple of weeks. After depositing my gear alongside a vacant cot next to his, Jody introduced me around and then disappeared on some errand.

Almost immediately after meeting the guys, I was knee deep in planning an air assault mission with the flight lead. The planning went on until after midnight. Throughout the night, Jody, who was too junior to really help out as a planner, kept bringing in coffee, food and everything else we needed. The next morning when I woke up and crawled out of my sleeping bag, he was already gone. He had been out collecting things like fresh coffee and more rolls, and had even made copies of the crew packets we had put together the evening before.

So it always went with Jody. When I became the chief pilot for the organisation, he was seldom further than a couple of metres away from anything that was going on and he flew anything he could to get flight time. I started to see him for what he was and, perhaps, what he might become. When young aviators go through flight school, they are told that when they finally get their first flying assignments, they should 'tuck up under the wing' of some 'crusty' old aviator. While I don't fancy myself as being crusty, Jody had definitely chosen me. For everything I taught him, he rewarded us with excellent performances of his ever-growing flying ability.

After a year, I had become great friends with Jody and his wife. One Saturday, during a cook-out at their house, Jody sprang his plan on me.

It was common knowledge I had spent a significant amount of time in the army's only special operations aviation regiment. I wore its combat patch boldly on my right sleeve. Jody told me that he wanted to join special ops and said he wanted me to teach him everything I could to prepare him.

Fate was hard at work that night. I had just created the first flight lead course for the 101st Airborne Division, the 'Screaming Eagles', and I was looking at assessing some highly-qualified aviators against my training regime. Was Jody ready? Could he even keep up? I decided to give him the chance. It was an unpopular decision, since many more senior pilots would be bypassed by this very junior pilot. I could write a book about Jody, and, perhaps someday, I will, but suffice to say, his performance during the intense training was nothing short of magnificent.

Soon afterwards, on a dark winter night, I knew for sure I had chosen wisely. I was riding in the jump seat while Jody and another flight lead trainee were flying a low-level route at about 300 feet in low illumination. Before any of us realised it, we had flown right into a blinding snow shower. When a pilot finds himself in what we call inadvertent IMC (instrument meteorological conditions), the procedure is to climb immediately, transition to instruments and continue in that manner at altitude. Unfortunately, this is not the best tactical option for a military pilot who wants to avoid being seen. Sometime earlier, when Jody and I had discussed the possibility, I told him that in such a situation, I would maintain altitude, execute a 180-degree turn and simply fly out of the weather.

You have to appreciate that I was speaking as a veteran of twenty years and more than 8,000 hours of flying. This night, the two guys in the front had only around 1,000 hours each, with Jody being the most junior. It's times like this when one appreciates one's own mortality. I was in danger and had absolutely no control of this helicopter. Jody said evenly, "I'm coming right; clear me," and smoothly turned that Chinook around. Within a minute, we had exited the shower and could see once again. Turning his head toward me, Jody told me that some crusty old pilot had taught him that trick. At that instant, I knew he was the one I had been looking for. I would pour my heart and soul into him, and I knew that in return, he would reward his army and nation many times over. He would become a great aviator and the kind of special leader we all look to in times of need.

During the next year, in which I retired, Jody was assessed for and was accepted into army special operations, where he became a flight lead in record time. Although I had left the army, I continued to hear from Jody every once in a while during the next few years.

Then, one day while I was driving back from the airport where I flew regional jets, I had the radio tuned to the public news channel. With my head still buzzing from the leg I had flown from the Bahamas to Cincinnati, I wasn't taking too much notice of what was being said. However, when I heard the newscaster announce that the army had lost an MH-47 helicopter, it focused pretty quickly. The regular army flies the CH-47 (meaning 'cargo helicopter'), but the MH-47 ('mission helicopter') is flown only by special ops guys.

I remember that moment as clearly as if I were looking at a photograph directly in front of me. I gripped the steering wheel tightly and uttered a prayer: "Please, God, don't let it be Jody." But it was one prayer that would not be answered. After I got back to my apartment, I almost didn't want to answer the phone when it rang. "Don," said the voice at the other end, "I have some bad news; it's Jody…he's gone." I still can't write or talk about it with a clear eye.

Jody's father asked me to speak at the service to honour his son. It seemed completely surreal to me as I stood there in front of hundreds of people. All around me and at the back of the church stood many comrades of Jody's and mine, all wearing their decorations, maroon berets and spit-shined boots. I tried to keep my jaw squared and my words even, but I could not, as I spoke of Jody's love of flying and his desire to serve his nation. I was mindful that the special training I had given Jody had got him into that unit. I felt I had to take some ownership for the very high price my friend and his crew had paid a couple of days earlier.

Standing there at the podium in that very crowded church, even as my mouth spoke the words I had penned straight from my heart, in my mind's eye, I pictured a little boy watching an F-4 Phantom fighter climbing towards the heavens.

Could anyone ever really divert a passion that is so deeply rooted in a man's soul? And even if we could, should we try? To what purpose? To save a life, perhaps? I think not. I believe you must make the best of what you have and strive for it with everything in your spirit. Grab life with both hands and don't let go. If, in doing so, it costs you your very life, perhaps it proves you *really* lived...To Jody.

Chapter 12

THE
THOUSAND-YARD
STARE

I know what it is like to love a woman so much that it physically hurts to walk away from her. I know what it is like to have a deep and abiding respect for my father and to admire him for the sacrifices in his life. I know what it costs to be honest – and the price you pay when you aren't. I know what it is like to see my reflection in my son's tear-filled eyes when I turn to leave to go off to war.

I know what it is to be so scared that you bite through your tongue and taste your own blood. I have had my last and final thought, only to survive a minute more and experience the elation of knowing I'm still alive. And I know what it is like to love my country even though some of my countrymen don't have a clue. I have learned of honour, loyalty, dedication, tradition and sacrifice.

I have met great men who knew no fear and I have watched lesser men run from danger. I have learned that the only real limits we have are self-imposed, that one's fears are one's greatest enemies, and to conquer them is to find freedom. And I have come to know my creator in a personal way.

I learned all these lessons along the path of being an army aviator and soldier – a path that certainly wasn't easy or profitable. Most people miss the lessons that such experience offers; they miss it by pursuing safer and more traditional paths, and I guess that's OK. But for me, there was only one course to take, and in doing so, I learned the most valuable lessons of all.

I think it all began with my father, a B-17 pilot in World War II. He was shot down, shot up and frozen nearly to death in an unheated, unpressurised aluminium war machine while lumbering along at 20,000 feet. Flak exploded all around him at times, and fighters searched for him and his fellow aviators, and sometimes found them. The losses of the 8th US Air Force were amongst the highest that any US Army unit ever sustained.

My father had a quiet confidence about him, and when he met another warrior, I noticed a special bond. It was the direct eye-to-eye contact, the firm handshake and the slap on the back. It was further evidenced by an occasional tear and hearty laughter. They spoke the names of others who had flags posted by their headstones; those names were always spoken about with the deepest respect.

Only occasionally would my father mention anything about the war; one really had to listen, and it always captivated me. Once, as I rummaged through a cedar chest of my Mom's, I found some black and whites of old aeroplanes. One was of the tail of an aeroplane taken in flight and even my youthful eyes could tell something wasn't right. The metal was torn and jagged, and a lot of it looked like the grid in my bedroom window. During supper that night, I presented the photo to Dad and asked him about it. He glanced at it and then went back to eating; it was his custom to never answer anything directly without first thinking about what he might say.

After supper, he took me into the living room and explained that the photo was one of his aeroplane taken in flight during the war. I remember it well because he stopped looking at me and adopted the same stare, fixed at infinity, that he sometimes adopted when talking with his veteran friends.

He talked as if I wasn't there.

"If you see flak, you need to be ready to feather the prop. If it is black, you just fly right through it. If it is red, you'd better check your engines right away; you are probably hit somewhere and if you lose oil pressure, you're in a little trouble. But, if you see orange, you are hit and you may only have seconds to get the prop feathered. If you don't and you lose all the oil, then that dead engine will create enough drag to cause you real trouble."

"Dad, did you ever lose an engine?"
"Son, I have lost many – far too many…"

Not all of my father's recollections were gloomy, but one never really knew how they were going to turn out until the end. He spoke of one mission when the flak had found him. German gunners had destroyed an engine over Germany and Dad's plane could no longer keep up with the formation. Two P-51s escorted his straggling bomber safely all the way back to England and the small airfield where the 351st Bomb Wing was stationed.

With the weather deteriorating as they arrived, the two P-51 pilots elected to land and spend the night and fly back to their own base in the morning. Dad put them both up in his building – a Quonset hut with a few spare bunks. They shared dinner and some drinks at the officers' club and traded stories, as is a common custom amongst aviators. The next morning, after listening to the Mustang pilots bragging about the performance of their sleek fighters, Dad watched them lift off from the runway. The first aircraft pulled up into a climb, but for no apparent reason, as the second fighter lifted off, it rolled inverted and crashed in a nearby stand of trees. That was the way a lot of his stories went – one minute a story might be of new-found friends and high adventure, and the next instant, it could change and leave one faced with stark reality and confronting the brevity of life.

That's how it is in combat. During the invasion of Panama – Operation Just Cause (we all called it 'just-cos') – I had the same kind of experience for the first time. It was either day two or three of the operation, it escapes me now, but US forces were moving close to the gulf side of the Panama Canal. The night before, I had flown two of a number of special operations missions by helicopters in preparation for the upcoming attack. As the battle for Colón began, our Little Birds (AH-6) began hammering Panamanian Defence Forces' targets with their mini guns and 2.75-inch rockets. The Chinooks that I was flying were ferrying ammunition, troops and fuel, and had set up a FARP nearby. The Little Bird gunships made frequent trips to the FARP to re-arm and occasionally take on fuel.

I flew my Chinook to Howard Air Force Base on the Pacific side to get some more of everything and returned around two hours later. When we got back, the Little Birds were no longer flying. At first, I thought we must have dispatched the enemy already, but I was very wrong. When I asked for an update, somebody told me that Sonny and Lieutenant Hunter had just been shot down and were presumed dead. The words hit me like a Mack truck. I remember looking at the soldier and saying, "Don't f**k with me; where are they?" The answer was unequivocal: "They're dead; they're just dead." That was it – and that's how it is. One minute you're on top of the world, everything is going well, and the next, something terrible happens.

Many years later, when I came back from my next war, I, too, had developed the same stare I had seen in my father. After much soul searching and rehashing of missions, it was my father who finally brought me home. With kindness and understanding, he talked me down and shared time with me for hours in the shade of the old chestnut tree in his back yard. Finally, he told me of his war. He spoke openly about men – his friends – dying, of the terrible destruction and the tumble of emotions one goes through after something like that. My Dad died a couple of years ago; an unsung American hero and part of what I think was our finest generation.

Occasionally, I see the same stares in Afghanistan, and I saw them in Iraq. There is a whole new generation of warriors taking its place in today's battles; some yearn to hear the sound of the big guns and some others really don't want to – but they all serve honourably, none the less.

This newest generation will also go home to raise their families quietly just like my Dad did, even after learning the same difficult and sometimes traumatic lessons. Their children might also stumble across pictures, perhaps of burned out Humvees or crashed aircraft, and ask their fathers to explain them. They will look into their eyes and struggle for ways to explain the unimaginable to innocent minds. They will fight back the emotion as they struggle with memories of losing friends and force smiles as they try to put such things into words in ways that don't really say what happened.

When my Dad was still around, he had always liked one of my best friends, Gerry Izzo. When my second son was born, my Dad called from Maryland and asked who was with me. When I told him the girls, my pastor and Gerry, he had asked me, "Do you mean Gerry Izzo? You know, I think he has always been there." It was true; Gerry always seemed to be around whether things were good or the chips were down.

Gerry was another American hero. He and I first met in 1980 in Kitzingen, Germany, and often flew together during our army careers and on special operations. One day, in 1993, I was driving home from Fort Campbell and stopped at an intersection. As I watched for a break in the oncoming traffic, as the last car approached, I could clearly see the driver had the thousand-yard stare of a man who has seen some really bad stuff, and it was my friend Gerry. I waved, but he was lost in whatever thought he was having and he drove right past me, immersed in his private world.

A couple of weeks earlier, Gerry had taken part in a battle in Mogadishu, Somalia, that was made infamous when enemy forces successfully shot down several of my unit's helicopters. CNN had repeatedly played footage of my friends being dragged through the streets of that city while their families had tried to deal with the loss. That combat had been some of the most intense ever seen by the US Army. Gerry had survived that day but, like my Dad, was changed forever. I don't know how many times he and I have talked about that time. Were the decisions right or wrong? Could things have turned out differently? I hate the second-guessing.

Allow me to tell a funny story about Gerry and me. As new pilots, we found ourselves assigned to the same unit in Germany – Alpha Company, 3rd Aviation Battalion, Combat, of the 3rd US Infantry Division. I flew the OH-58A Kiowa, which we used as an aeroscout platform, and Gerry was a command pilot in a UH-1H Huey and had a rock solid reputation. It was a great first unit to be in; it boasted forty aircraft and had a seemingly unlimited flight hour programme. I had become a border-qualified scout and was authorised to fly right up to the sensitive border between East and West Germany.

On this particular day, I was flying as a co-pilot for Gerry in a Huey. I was not current in the Huey, but the fact that I was border qualified put me in the right seat on a reconnaissance flight of the border. While flying near Checkpoint 23, we heard a mayday call on the guard frequency. The mayday call was surreal: "Mayday, Mayday, Red Catcher 55 is under attack." (Red Catcher was the call sign for all 2nd Armoured Cavalry units.)

The controlling agency radioed back asking for his position and a situation report. Gerry and I looked at each other and continued to listen. "This is Red Catcher 55. I am in the vicinity of Checkpoint 25. I am being attacked by a Mi-8 Echo." Hearing that, I cranked the Huey over, and accelerated to VNE and headed directly towards Checkpoint 25.

From the back of our helicopter, the cavalry squadron commander, Lieutenant-Colonel Steel, yelled at us to get over there as quickly as we could. Gerry asked me what my plan was and what I intended to do. Without thinking it through, I told him: "We're going to draw his fire and give Red Catcher a chance to escape!"

It took Gerry a couple of seconds to reply, but his reply was classic: "We're going to do what?" You should have seen his face! Yes, I know it was not the best of plans, but that's how it played out. As we approached the area, we saw an Mi-8 making slow passes over the OH-58. It looked like the East German was just playing around, but I can appreciate that it must have been pretty scary for the Cav pilot, not knowing if the Hip was going to shoot.

Thankfully, before we had to do anything, Gerry saw two F-4 Phantoms smoking up the valley so we cleared off. The air force had launched the Phantoms out of Ramstein Air Base to either intercept the Hip or shoot it down.

After seeing those Phantoms come streaking by, the Hip pilot popped back across the border into East Germany and ended the incident.

Such is every military aviator's life, one of constantly mixed emotions. He will experience the highest of thrills and the lowest of lows. He will be scared, happy, lonely, unsure, tired, hungry, angry and have a hundred other feelings. Over time, he will become part of an elite group who place their personal wants and desires second to the needs of their nation. However tough the life might be, no military aviator ever wants to walk away from it. I think the best description I have ever heard of a military aviator's thinking came in the closing of a recent letter from a friend. It said:

There are only two things an army aviator really fears. The first is taking off not knowing if it might be his last flight, and the second is taking off knowing it is to be his last flight.

Chapter 13

DÉJÀ-VU

The other day, we were racing across the desert at fifty feet. The airspeed indicator read a comfortable 135 knots and the rotor blades were smoothly doing whatever they do up there, going round and round. We were in the number two position at an extended forty-five-degree angle from lead on the left side. I was on the controls and was keeping us at about a quarter mile spacing; close enough to keep lead in sight, but far enough away so as not to provide a juicy target for some guy on the other team.

I like flying 'cross panel' – looking across the cockpit and out of the other pilot's windshield at the other aircraft – because it allows me an occasional quick scan of the instruments while maximising the time I spend looking outside. Flying at that airspeed and altitude, one is pretty safe from fast little metallic flying things but only half a hiccup away from becoming a flaming ball of aluminium; it's a fun little balancing act between the right and left edges of human existence.

This reminds me of something I heard one of my combat medics say a couple years ago as we raced to transport a wounded patient to a CSH (combat army surgical hospital). When I noticed that the usual frenzy of activity in the back had stopped and the guys were just looking out either side of the aircraft, I asked how the patient was doing. The medic paused briefly and simply said, "His injuries were inconsistent with life!" Think about that for a moment... Isn't that sobering? Back in the present, I realised that hitting the ground at the speed we were travelling would produce exactly the same results.

The leg we were flying was a routine one at just under an hour. When I say 'routine', keep in mind that, unlike the airline guys who can sit back and check their stocks while cruising along at flight level three seven zero, ours is hands-on stick-and-rudder flying, second by exciting second. Even so, it is not always exciting enough to keep the mind from occasionally wandering and in a moment of déjà-vu, while my view outside stayed the same, in my mind, it all suddenly changed. As my aircraft vibrated heavily from the six massive rotor blades beating over my head, I was suddenly back in a hot and sweaty Chinook in another, different desert and another desert war.

My mind recalled the old sounds, feelings and smells of our MH-47 as we raced across that earlier desert at breakneck speed towards southern Iraq. We had three pilots in the cockpit – I was the mission commander and Dave was flying the aircraft. A third pilot sat in the jump seat behind us with the sole task of monitoring our altitude; if it dropped below seventy-five feet, it was his job to call: "Climb, climb, climb!" If the pilot on the controls did not respond immediately, he was tasked to reach forward and pull the collective up to save our lives!

The mission was a hairy one. It was night-time and the weather was awful, with a ceiling of barely 100 feet and half a mile visibility. Despite the conditions, we had the proverbial pedal to the metal as we raced northwards to try to save a downed air force pilot. According to his wingman, their flight had been launched upon by an SA-6. This is a particularly nasty surface-to-air missile that will hunt you down and absolutely kill you. The wingman had witnessed the missile actually strike his leader's F-16 and blow the back end completely off his plane.

That was the bad news. The good news was that the front half had survived with a precious American life still on board; the pilot had pulled the 'Hail Mary' handle and ejected. Less fortunately, although the F-16 pilot had survived the missile strike and subsequent ejection, he had landed very close to the guys who had shot him down.

I was the standby CSAR pilot that night and was, well, standing by when I got a message to go and see the colonel. I walked into Lieutenant Colonel Bailey's office to find the executive officer waiting for me. "Don, he's waiting for you in ops; get over there right away." I entered the classified area to find Colonel Bailey and the intelligence officer looking at a computer monitor. As I joined them, the intelligence officer recognised me and started explaining what had just happened almost 300 miles away. As he explained what everything was, I quickly noticed there were a lot of enemies packed onto that screen, and no friendlies. Then his finger tapped on a little dot on the screen.

"We think that's our man," he said, looking at me.

Colonel Bailey was an excellent commander with a hardcore ranger back-bone, the mind of a Rhodes scholar and the heart of a loving father. He searched me with a stare that settled everything in my mind. His strongest trait was an uncanny ability to really know his men and after our many desert experiences, he knew me well also. He simply said: "Don, I'm not going to order you to do this one." He paused to allow his words to sink in, then he continued. "But I'm not going to stop you either!"

The weight of those words was massive; I realised that this wasn't about me. This was the real deal; it was the very reason I was an officer – the moment of reckoning that every warrior wants and dreads, all at the same time. I had a crew 'to consider'. As well as the three pilots, there were three gunners, three 'long-hair types' (special forces troops who are encouraged to go against army norms and grow their hair and beards in order to help keep their identities secret) and three combat medics from another armed service. If we were to go, Colonel Bailey would also send two Blackhawks to shoot our way in to the pickup point. If I said yes, then perhaps some, or possibly all, of those people might not be coming home that night – including me. The decision was mine alone to make. I respectfully asked for a moment and left the room.

Officially, I was in charge. However, anyone who knows anything about the military also knows that its non-commissioned officers are its strength and backbone. I went straight to George, a special forces master sergeant and a veteran of special operations in Vietnam, and more than twenty years of hard army living. Even though I was officially in charge, I was not as 'blooded' as George. He had seen more than his share of war and had 'been there' far more often than I had. Tonight was probably going to be a tough mission. George commanded a tremendous amount of respect from all of us, and his wisdom and judgment were unquestionable.

Everyone's eyes followed us as we walked outside. I carefully explained the situation to George. After I gave him everything I had, he kicked the dirt around with his boots, thought for a moment, and looked me straight in the eyes. "Sir, I don't know about you, but I sure wouldn't want to be on the ground up there all alone."

We locked eyes as I weighed his words carefully: "OK, George; it's a go. Get the crew and aircraft ready; I'm going back to ops."

"Roger that, Sir," he replied, and gave me a firm slap on my shoulder.

Here's how we looked at it. If this were to be our last mission, we would make our last few hours or minutes, or whatever, truly honourable. If this were to be our day of days then we would do it as men, with our heads held high.

I thought back to the speech of Russ Carmody again, who was my company commander at the time. I remembered we were specially selected and carefully trained to become our nation's silent warriors. He was the consummate warrior and a dammed good leader, and his pilots were 'his boys'. With his words in my mind, it was as if my heart were tattooed with the red, white and blue flag; it swelled with resolve and I was able to make that important, necessary switch in gears that told me it was about others and not about me.

I told Colonel Bailey we were going to give it a try. Grabbing my hand to shake it, he simply said, "God speed, Don. Go get him."

A couple of hours later, it was a hell of a mess, there was no other way to describe it. The situation in the target area had deteriorated to the extent that with so much steel being put into the air by anti-aircraft fire, the other F-16s had to bug out. However, the air force guys wouldn't give up. Other fighter pilots continued to drop bombs in an attempt to 'soften up' the area that they knew would soon be crossed by helicopters making a desperate attempt to get their guy. An air force MH-53 'Pave Low' special operations helicopter was busy making its way to the target area from a different direction, while we were 'threading the eye of the needle'.

An airborne platform directed our flight through the various obstacles, and our crews were at their limits dealing with the terrible weather and visibility, and the enemy situation. Our MH-47 had a FLIR (forward looking infrared), which wasn't doing a particularly good job of seeing through the dense fog. Our NVGs (night vision goggles) were also at their limits, since it was darker than the inside of a bucket of black paint. About all we could see was the ground just below the aircraft, and virtually nothing in front. Despite this, we were pushing it along at around 140 knots. Although the weather was bad, we knew the sun would be up in a couple of hours and we would be sitting ducks. We had very little time to prosecute this mission and 'get the hell out of Dodge'.

Rather unexpectedly, the Pave Low reported arrival over the target. Those guys were getting shot at by everything. Looking at our mission computer, we knew we would also be there soon. We got a call from Colonel Bailey who ordered us to land where we were and await further orders; the plan was changing rapidly. Because the Pave Low was taking so much fire, it was feared that it too would get shot down, leaving only us to pick everyone up. We landed in the middle of nowhere and the two Blackhawks landed one on either side of us. The long hair guys alighted and immediately set up a perimeter a couple of hundred metres away. Through their headsets, they communicated the ground situation back to us.

Everyone listened to the battle frequency on Satcom (satellite communications radio) as the Pave Low tried repeatedly to get to the downed air force pilot. Eventually, we heard the call that made me sick; the F–16 guy had probably only had a ten percent chance of making it in the first place and his luck had just run out. The call to return to base was an emotional low-of-lows for us. We had put everything on the line and flown in the worst conditions any of us had ever seen, but in spite of all that effort, we had lost him anyway and were coming home empty handed.

Later, after sunrise, we rendezvoused with the Pave Low guys at a forward base. The downed pilot had been talking to them on his survival radio. As they tried to locate him amidst all the mayhem, they heard him say, "They got me; they got me. Get the hell out of here!" I can hardly remember the rest of the mission, but for some reason, remember other inconsequential things. For example, I remember that after talking to the Pave guys, I sat down on the floor beside a big green air conditioning unit bearing a brass plate that said 'Trane Corporation, Clarksville, Tennessee'. By irrelevant coincidence, at that time, I actually lived in Clarksville, Tennessee.

Only a few weeks after this mission, I was back home in the US. As I flew across the Appalachian mountains north of Asheville, North Carolina, my head was still in some sort of wacky transition between there and Iraq. The crew I was flying with hadn't been over for desert fun, but were getting ready to go. I don't know why, but for some reason, they must have been talking about tactics, when someone said the words 'taking fire' on the intercom. Whatever they were talking about, those were the only words I heard.

In a split second, I had that aircraft in a sixty-degree bank and about two ball-widths out of trim. I aimed for a narrow draw to my right, sure in the knowledge that if I could just have two or three more seconds, I could get our giant Chinook down into that narrow valley and we might just escape. As I clawed for the ground in a crazy emergency descent, rolling ever more steeply, it suddenly occurred to me that this was North Carolina. Slowly, I rolled the aircraft level, increased power for a climb and placed the aircraft in trim. My heart was doing about 170 beats a minute. I took a couple of deep breaths, looked over at my co-pilot and said: "You have the controls."

He had one of those 'What the heck was that?' looks on his face and one of the crew chiefs in the back was saying, "Big Don, it's OK; it's OK. No one is shooting at us. I'm sorry." I drew another breath. "Please, don't ever do that again." For most of the rest of the flight, almost no one spoke. Later that night, I heard them talking about how they thought I was still in the war and was wrapped way too tight. They were absolutely right.

I was undoubtedly suffering from some stress-related syndrome, which I am sure some psychologist could name, but I didn't care. I knew that healing could be found under an ancient chestnut tree in Maryland. There, a week later, I sat in an old homemade wooden chair and listened to my father. As the wind blew gently through the branches and spring leaves above us, slowly and with the skill of a surgeon, his measured words finally brought me back home and away from that war.

Chapter 14

TWO DAYS
IN AUGUST

Every time I turn on my computer, I am immediately greeted by a picture of my wife or my boys. I set it up that way so that I am constantly reminded of what is important to me, and to put my life and all that is happening around me, into perspective; it is such a stark contrast to the everyday lives of the people all around me here in Afghanistan.

DAY ONE

Something was going on that first day; something dangerous. I picked up a sense of it during the morning briefing. The face of the young man who normally gave us the 'threat' portion of the briefing was drawn with deep lines that reflected great concern, and very little sleep. He looked much older than his twenty-four years. As he pointed out known enemy positions and the various corridors we should use to stay away from 'hot spots' – and I do not refer to weather – I could tell he was distracted by something else.

After our briefing was over, I downed the last of my coffee as I waited until the briefer was free, and then approached him. I sensed that we were, or were about to be, in the middle of something big.

"The TIC (troops in contact) up north is bad, isn't it?" I asked him. He could see the genuine concern on my face. "Yes, sir. It's bad. Real bad. We thought we had an MIA (missing in action), but it looks like the pile of body parts over there could be one of the soldiers." He continued as if it somehow made sense to him; after all, he was an analyst. "I guess that during the confusion, after the second IED went off, while they were looking for the first guy, we had another guy captured."

The seriousness of the situation really hit home. "We just found him," the analyst continued, "but they'd killed him soon after they captured him. I guess they don't want any prisoners." He stopped talking; his mind wasn't really there, anyway. He was trying to suppress all the same emotions of the sadness and anger that I was feeling at that moment. I thought about the pictures of my sons — one with a carefree smile and the other with an expression which said: "But, Dad, I didn't do it." That world was so very far away right at that moment.

As we drove out to the flight line, there was more evidence something was going on. Through the dust hanging over the road, I saw a medevac Blackhawk helicopter racing straight across the airfield heading directly for the hospital. It wasn't slowing down as they normally did, but was racing straight for the red and white pad. My mind wandered back to some of the times when I, too, had been that pilot, desperately trying to squeeze another one or two knots of speed out of the helicopter to give the poor guy in the back a better chance. That's when I remembered the 'medical pad condition' slide from the briefing. It had been showing amber in colour, which meant the hospital was nearing capacity. Either this TIC must have been going on for some time or our guys had got themselves into a real hornet's nest.

Morning briefings normally told us things like that to give us some idea of what to expect in case we suddenly needed to become medevac birds ourselves, and, if we did, whether the hospital could actually take new casualties. As far as I was concerned, though, if there were a guy in the back hanging onto life, I was always going to head for the nearest and best facility available, regardless.

As we ran through our routine pre-flight and crew briefing, I watched a Mirage fighter jet taking off with a deafening roar from its turbojet engine. As I looked over to watch the number two aircraft take off, I noticed a heavy payload of bombs slung under its wings. After take-off, the two jets turned north, directly towards the area of the TIC. Everything I saw suggested a sense of urgency. I was beginning to wonder if the day's activities would turn out much different from what I was anticipating. The Mirages' take-off was almost a routine thing for that time of the morning, but what wasn't routine was a second pair of aircraft, Air Force A-10 Thunderbolts, that departed shortly afterwards; the fearsome Thunderbolt, with its GAU-30 belly-mounted 30-mm cannon is used in the close air support role. Like the preceding Mirages, the two Thunderbolts also banked sharply northward after take-off. Also like the Mirages, their engines were not throttled back.

I didn't know it at the time, but the situation only a few miles north of us was much worse than I had imagined. As I stood watching those aircraft depart, we had already lost several brave young men and many more had been wounded. Although it was not my mission to go there, I kept the part of the briefing about 'safe corridors' in mind just in case we got an unexpected mission change and were directed to go there and assist.

Shortly after pulling pitch on our first take-off, we heard that now all-too-familiar radio call: "Tower _____ [call sign deleted]. Flight of two Blackhawks inbound. Urgent medevac." The voice was female. It was strained and holding back a ton of emotion. I knew what was going on in the back of her bird, and in her mind. Other pilots will always clear the area when they hear that call to give medevac pilots a clear run to where they need to go.

Our initial turn was to the north-northeast. Immediately after clearing the traffic pattern, we flew past a flight of Kiowa-armed reconnaissance helicopters. They were also heading north. Their wing stores were full and they were heading into a fight. We only travelled a couple more miles before we had to turn to avoid a flight of Apache gunships going back to the FARP.

As we cleared the airport traffic area and began climbing to what I had picked as the safest mission altitude, we switched our radio to our assigned tactical frequencies. As we did, the radio was suddenly awash with traffic. 'Backlash' – the call sign for the guy running the show – was flooded by a constant exchange between low-level helicopters, and mid- and high-level fighters, tankers and even bombers. Everyone was involved in this show.

I knew it wasn't going to be easy to get a word in edgeways, so I was very brief as I squeezed the transmit trigger.

"Backlash, this is Slapper." This guy was busy but sharp.

"Slapper, Backlash, standby. Break; break. Reaper flight. Clear to elevate one niner five. Contact Lockjaw on blue two niner." And then immediately, "Slapper, Backlash, go ahead."

"Backlash, Slapper. Transition 26 Foxtrot to 89 Quebec, 5,000; over."

"Slapper, Backlash. Cleared as requested. Avoid ROZ (restricted operating zone) Nathaniel by ten miles."

Looking down at my map, I could see ROZ Nathaniel just to our north. "Roger Backlash." Whatever in hell's name was going on up there, it was starting to sound like the beginning of World War III!

We did turns for seven hours that day, hauling out all sorts of cargo and troops to various locations all around our central base. All day, the radio traffic never ended, the fighters never stopped sortieing, and the medevacs never stopped coming and going.

At one point, when I was refuelling my aircraft, I got out to stretch my legs. I walked a short distance away from the aircraft and as I pulled off my helmet, I heard the 'boom, boom, boom' sound of outgoing artillery. Then I heard the 'crump, crump, crump' as those rounds found their mark around twenty seconds later. The sound came from the north.

DAY TWO

The following morning, we again found ourselves in the TOC (tactical operations centre) where the same tired army specialist and captain gave us their portion of the daily briefing. Much like the day before, there was significant activity just to our north. These guys looked like crap. Their faces were masks of fatigue, expressionless and drained. Later, I learned that the young captain had not had any sleep in forty hours. Last night must have been hell for him. He was running on sheer will power; there was nothing left.

Again, I cornered the intelligence guy. "How'd our guys do? Did we get hurt?" Again, he studied my face and answered rather matter-of-factly: "Yes, sir, we got hurt." He did not turn away but just stood there staring at me. It was as if he had fallen asleep – while standing up with his eyes open. I left that briefing room saddened and concerned. Today, we would be flying to the FOB where the fighting had just taken place.

The day had already been long and very hot by the time we arrived; it had been over 100 degrees Fahrenheit since just a little after sunrise. We had been in our cockpits since soon after finishing all of the typical early morning briefings, making numerous runs to various FOBs. Ours and other aircraft were carrying a lot of stuff up to that forward base, and taking a lot of tired-looking troops and others back to our main base. So far, we had already logged more than six hours and still had work to do.

The hastily-built ramp at the FOB was surfaced with purpose-designed metal plates laid over levelled gravel-covered desert. We had to taxi between two running aircraft, a Chinook and a Mil-8, but in such places, this is 'business as usual'.

Sitting there on the aluminium panels beside the gravel, I slowed the engines to idle to minimise the noise and rotor blast as I busied myself filling out the trip log with flight times for each leg, fuel used, loads carried and other information. The ramp was a beehive of activity with all sorts of people hustling about, loading and unloading helicopters, and sagging under the load of huge rucksacks.

Everyone was moving except for three soldiers who were standing next to some largish plastic or metal boxes. The way they stood there was different enough to make me look a second time. That's when I noticed they weren't wearing helmets, vests or protection of any kind. They were expressionless, just like the battle captain and specialist had been when they briefed us. They were in a transformed state, no longer a complete part of reality. They had seen or experienced something terrible.

As the men stood motionless, staring at me, I recognised something else, something familiar. Their faces were covered with dirt, as were their uniforms. As I took another look at the scene…and those boxes – I realised what it was that I was looking at. Releasing the cyclic, I lifted the shaded visor covering my face so that I could raise my right arm slowly and render a heartfelt salute. Slowly and deliberately, one of the men straightened and returned my salute.

A moment later, it was time to go. Before taxiing away, I turned one last time towards the soldiers and nodded. It was a nod of respect. Standing there with all that was left in the world of their friends, they nodded back as I taxied away but otherwise, they didn't move.

For some reason, when a man dies, his possessions become hallowed. A previously worthless item can become a focal point for people's emotions. A simple touch of the dog tags can bring grown men or women to their knees; I have seen it happen. We humans do not like to let go of loved ones; suddenly, we are interested in a person's every little possession, as if they were doorways providing some mystical insight into the soul.

The brotherhood that forms between soldiers amid the terror and misery of war can be amongst the strongest of human bonds. The friends I have made in such times become more than trusted and the bonds we have formed almost transcend those of family.

The friends I have buried are my personal saints. Those soldiers on that hot dusty pickup zone, standing watch over their friends' possessions, were just starting that emotional journey.

Chapter 15

THE JOURNEY

A friend of mine, Gerry, said something the other day that stuck in my head. We were getting ready to go flying on Thanksgiving Day and were pre-flighting the aircraft. He and I have both flown various helicopters and jets during our careers. Looking at the modern lines of our AgustaWestland AW139, he said, "You know, with airplanes, it's about the destination; but with helicopters, it's about the journey."

Gerry's words certainly struck a chord and they started me thinking. When flying jets, you are always 'parked' on some airway miles above the surface watching while the autopilot flies the aircraft precisely to a point when ATC starts squawking at you to descend. But with helicopters, you remain connected with the earth; it is never all that far away. Sometimes it is 1,000 feet below, while at other times, it's just a few scant metres beneath the gear.

When I was driving Canadair regional jets around my corner of the globe, I remember listening to another Gerry; one whom I have written about here before. He was relating the circumstances of an 'emergency' that had happened to him. He said "Yeah; when we turned final to…one-eight right – or two-two right at Chicago…or maybe Cincinnati? Heck; I can't remember which one. Well, anyway…"

And that's how it is with jet flying. No one ever remembers where something happened; they only remember the incident itself. Why, you ask? Because every airport is the same. They're all just big pieces of concrete with nasty jets and vehicles scurrying around the outside of some enormous dirty buildings… all the same. In any given week, I might land in the Bahamas, in Canada and all over the US – and it was always all the same. I'd disembark the passengers, do a quick walk around, refuel, get back in my seat, do some paperwork, punch some numbers into a computer…You get the idea.Yes, it might be hot and humid in Nassau, and cold and breezy in Denver, but it is still just the same; trade palm trees for pine trees and throw in some mountains and *voila*!

With helicopters, you do not go from VOR to VOR, from airway to intersection to airway. No; you go from this bend in the river to that gap in the mountains in the distance, turn left up the valley and look for an airport on its right side near the smaller peak. Along the way, instead of taking that big gap, perhaps you might bend the thing over a little more steeply and take the narrower gap further to the right instead. Heaven forbid that there might be some girls sunbathing beside the river – now we're talking: 'automatic low fuel warning!'

Helicopter flying lets you see more of the world and to stay connected to it in a more personal way. I have heard my Harley-Davidson biker friends say the same thing about driving the open road astride eighty-eight inches of Milwaukee muscle compared to driving the same route in a cushy SUV. The Harley, blasting out its distinctive melody to travel, puts you point blank in the middle of it all: in control but still 'out there'. By comparison, the SUV affords you the opportunity to span the distance virtually in REM sleep.Yeah, I get that. To fail to get it would tell me I was not experiencing all that life has to offer.

Flying over the world at low level has afforded me some fairly remarkable views – and a million still-vivid memories. Like the day I rushed across the desert at around fifty feet before crossing over the edge of the Grand Canyon. In an instant, the world fell away to more than a mile below me. It was such an exhilarating experience; the canyon walls were ablaze with colour, and I felt like I was a part of it.

Then there was the time when I crossed over the Main river valley in central Germany one foggy morning. The valley below my trusty JetRanger was like white cotton, brilliantly illuminated by a rising sun in a cloudless autumn sky. The feeling of peace and serenity it conveyed was overpowering. And yet it was right there. I actually dipped down a little to skim through the top of it, watching church steeples and towers pass by.The feeling was like one of floating in a calm sea without a care in the world – secure and buoyant, resting on those calm white rivers of mist.

"It's about the journey and not the destination." The words just keep running round and round in my head. Doesn't that sum up life itself? Isn't it really all about the thousands of little moments in which we really live – really experience things – and not about the big rewards or vacation home or dream car? Indeed it is, and for some reason, in my mind, the two have become connected in a real sense – the two, being helicopter flying and the journey.

My journey through life has seen me in the front seats of a multitude of flying machines for many thousands of hours, through decades, over most of the planet's continents in times of war and in peace. It has changed the way I look at things. I don't see the sides of a mountain; I see the scattered rubble on its peak, and its sides sloping down and away. I don't see a bend in the river; I see a living thing coming from a distant ridgeline and passing forty miles away into the sea – a hapless snake meandering its way across the landscape. I wonder: does the place we helicopter pilots inhabit in our work somehow modify the way we think? Who knows? The answers are the stuff of psychology and philosophy. Nevertheless, when I think of my 'calling' – for what else would any real pilot call it? – I see a direct correlation between each journey and the experience of human life itself.

I remember a Thanksgiving Day journey far from home that took me to several outlying US bases during the course of eight sorties. We carried men and supplies, mail, boxes of every size, tools and all sorts of equipment. As we skimmed along ridgelines and flew high across valleys, my mind drifted to my home back in Kentucky. There, many thousands of miles away from this hostile place, I knew my family would soon gather over a grand walnut and mahogany table in a seldom-used dining room in my home to share a meal together. I pictured my boys talking loudly and playing with their mashed potatoes and gravy, and the girls being the perfect ladies they are so much of the time. I could picture my wife at the head of the table watching over them with a loving smile borne of so many shared experiences with all of them. I could almost hear them laughing and talking, chatting happily about nothing in particular, and I knew they would be thinking of me. My family has endured many Thanksgivings without me at the table, so it has become somewhat normal for my wife to lead the event – something I liken to 'herding cats'. But in my mind's eye, I could see them all as clearly as if I were seated at the other end of the table – the end where I would normally be doing a mediocre job of carving a great turkey. I would be looking outward at eyes full of anticipation of the great meal we were about to share. The boys would be feigning starvation, and the girls would be wearing a mixed bag of smiles and a look that says: "Are you ever going to get that thing cut apart?"

Such is the journey of life; it's found in a million moments just like that. But for soldiers, those moments are mostly solitary in nature. My family can't be here with me; nor would I want them to be. Heather often asks me to describe things about the war but when I try to, I realise I actually can't. You see, my journey is so different from their domestic life that I struggle to find the right words to explain.

My journey connects me to this place and, at the same time, separates me from those who matter the most. The voyage that acquaints me with the colour of the rocks and the knowledge of where that next valley leads also keeps me on a course that disconnects me from another journey – that of my family and loved ones. What a strange existence I have come to call 'normal'.

Despite being separated from my family, again, this Thanksgiving Day journey was good to me; very good indeed. If I cannot be with the ones I love, then let me be with others who really matter – our nation's selfless warriors. I had that opportunity this Thanksgiving Day and took it. The timing of our mission just happened to put us in the vicinity of a good-sized US camp at around noon, so we swung in there for Thanksgiving dinner. We parked our three aircraft alongside the fuel pits where giant bags of jet fuel lay protected behind a boundary of dirt and rock. As the throttles were closed and the rotors slowed to a stop, about a dozen eager air crewmen stumbled out of their aircraft, not used to standing on the uneven rocks of the helicopter landing area. We had already been sitting in our cockpits for more than five hours this day, so it was a very welcome break.

A short walk took us to a line leading into the dining facility. As the line grew shorter, the smell of freshly-cooked turkey and ham grew ever stronger. Inside was the sound of hundreds of happy soldiers, airmen and marines, as well as soldiers from other nations. The sight inside was one to remember. The cooks had done a fantastic job on both the setup and the actual food. There were life-sized bread statues, cake-shaped 'horns of plenty', fruits, desserts, drinks and sides of everything imaginable arrayed from wall to wall.

A few days earlier, I had actually delivered 600 lbs of frozen turkey to this very outpost; now it was my turn to enjoy the fruits of that labour. We all sat down at a long table and began to savour the rich traditional American food. The Romanians were picking through it but enjoying it just the same. We were joined by an air force captain wearing a flight suit identifying him as an MH-60 Pave Hawk pilot, while a soldier from the 82nd Airborne Division sat across from me with several pieces of pie, all smothered in Baskin Robbins ice cream. We all laughed and joked and thanked the Lord for such an amazing meal – relishing the tranquillity of a little piece of America confined within the deadly hills of central Afghanistan. We all knew it might turn out much differently later in the day, but for a short time, it was indeed heaven on earth.

I could hardly eat two bites without thinking of home. I drifted again. Now as my mind's eye stared past my wife's blonde hair to the fire in the hearth, the distinctive smell of hickory logs snapping and popping in the fireplace mixed with that of the meal, making me feel like it was a hundred years earlier in a log cabin. Above the brass pots on the hearth, I could see a framed photograph of all of us taken a couple of years earlier. Below me at my feet, Jack, our husky, sat impatiently waiting for me to sneak him a morsel or two when no one was looking.

These thoughts came with such realism and intensity that I could almost touch them. All too soon, our meal was over and it was time to walk back to our birds. Time again to crank those powerful engines, make the blades disappear in a whirl above our heads and turn some more jet gas into noise!

As we left the base, we turned north up into a narrow alpine valley that followed a stream and we passed several villages of mud and stone huts. Above us, the peaks were already covered in white after their first dusting of the impending winter's snow. Our next destination was a lonely outpost occupied by special forces soldiers where we had dropped off a couple of army chaplains earlier that morning. Having shared blessings and a meal with the troops stationed there, they were now awaiting pickup by our aircraft. As I looked at my watch, I realised our timing was perfect, it was 1430 and we had ten minutes to run to our scheduled pickup time of 1440.

That particular valley was very picturesque. Situated some 7,000 feet above sea level, with ridges well over 10,000 feet high on either side, it had a sandy sage colour. The rocks looked tortured, as does much of the terrain here, running from black to chocolate in colour. There were no real roads, just animal trails, and a path I would have loved to negotiate with my four-wheel drive. The stream in the centre of the valley was crystal clear and moving with some speed between clear pools dotted amidst the rocky rapids. For all its beauty, it was not a safe place. Recently, our soldiers had met the Taliban there in a bloody clash. Such is the way of this place; naked beauty overlaid by a deadly war of high technology and twelfth century idealism.

With a northerly wind swirling all around lower in the valley, we had made our approach from the south in the morning. Taking the principles of tactical surprise and diversity into consideration, we peeled out of the formation in a diving right turn and quickly disappeared behind a ridge. Lead and I would land, while 'Three' went high and circled to look for anything that that might surprise us.

My thought was to mix it up and approach from the east, turning into the wind only in the last 200 metres. Lead flew up the left side of the valley away from the village and made a straight-in approach. I came in at ninety degrees to him and turned onto final to land about 100 metres to his right on the hard rocky soil of the LZ. The dust cloud built quickly but passed well behind the other aircraft. We kept the rotors turning at 100 percent, giving us the ability to 'didimau' ('go quickly') just in case someone decided to drop a mortar shell on us.

A Toyota Hilux and a heavily-armoured Hummer drove up with our passengers. A gruff-looking, bearded soldier got out of the truck and walked to the front of the car. He was wearing ACU (army combat uniform) pants combined with local garb and had a cigar stuffed in the side of his mouth; special forces guys start looking pretty wild when left in remote places for too long. He shook hands with the two chaplains then turned to look at us. Seeing us return his look directly, he gave us a salute with two fingers – more of a wave, actually – before turning and walking away. It was the language of soldiers; a casual acknowledgement between fellow warriors. He had probably seen our approach and knew that we 'knew'. With our passengers safely aboard, we took off while Chalk Three covered our departure from above.

In short order, we were back in the cruise mode on our way home on our final leg of the day. The turkey was beginning to take effect on all of us. There was no silly chatter on the radio and none within our cockpit either. People were tired; with bellies full, we were ready for a nap.

I swung into a tight echelon right to check out a panel on lead's aircraft that looked to be open. It wasn't, so I dived away to the right and then corrected sharply back to the left. Pat looked over at me for a moment after the jink as if I had interrupted his rest, then turned back to look out the left side of the bird.

I was just beginning to drift back to that table in Kentucky when I noticed a plume of rising smoke to the left of lead. I was studying it, realising there was nothing there to burn, when I saw the second explosion; this time, it registered in my conscious mind. "Lead! Explosions left. Break right!"

"Roger that. In sight," he responded, breaking right, away from the area of rising rocks and debris. None of us knew who, why or what the explosions were all about. Perhaps someone was just pissed off at some rocks; we didn't care; I didn't care. It was Thanksgiving and no one was going to take that away from me.

My mind drifted slowly back to Kentucky – back to that safe place where another part of my journey waited quietly and patiently.

Chapter 16

NICKNAMES

Nicknames: aviators sure have some good ones. We aviators aren't all that smart and we tend towards simple, easy names. There are the standard ones like 'Meat' and 'Hammer' and 'Big-' …anything; then there are the other ones. That is where the stories lie, in the particular circumstances that conspired to create the situations that justified them. Whether one is lucky to get a good nickname, or unfortunate in getting a less flattering one, nicknames can follow an aviator for a lifetime.

Once you have earned 'Meat', then you're probably always going to be known as such. You'll undoubtedly get derivatives of the original from time to time. For example, your commander might find the term 'Meat-head' to be very handy should he wish to make an example of your inadequacies to others: "You're not Meat-head; from now on, you're 'Bone-head!'" But in the end, your name will inevitably revert back simply to 'Meat'. "Yeah; I remember when Meat took those rounds over at…" The story endures; the names live on.

My fate was to be given the 'Big-' nickname. Being six-feet three-inches tall pretty much guaranteed that, but a decision by the army in 1980 placed the icing on the cake. Fresh out of flight school, about a century and a half ago, I was made an aeroscout. Back then, the 'Big Green Machine' used the venerable (and terrible) JetRanger, which the army designated the OH-58A Kiowa. It was an under-powered adaptation of the highly-successful Bell JetRanger that the army had overburdened with armour, extra fuel, electronic gear we did not need and a bunch of other junk. It was a smallish aircraft with non-adjustable nylon mesh seats that fitted pilots who were about five-feet eight-inches tall. I was way over-qualified in the height department, so I became an object of amusement

for the mechanics and crew chiefs that made comments about the big guy stuff-
ing himself into the tiny helicopter. Once, a mechanic left a salt and pepper
shaker on the seat for me. The implication was that because my knees were
nearly in my face, I might as well season them to make them taste better. Thus,
almost from the first, it was 'Big Don', a name which follows me still.

I suppose I ought to be thankful for being allowed to have at least part of my
real name; others are not always so fortunate. You see, nicknames are bestowed
by others and never chosen by their owners. They are often earned as the results
of hopelessly stupid acts, which their new namesakes were fortunate to have survived. Take Matt, for example. If you heard Matt on the phone, you'd think he
was ten-feet tall and bulletproof; he certainly wasn't. God had given him maybe
five-feet six-inches and not a tenth more. Guys of his build have to compensate
somehow, especially in the testosterone-rich environment in which we worked
back then. In the ranks of Type A-plus personality special operations pilots, this
required an abnormally large adjustment to the voice volume regulator. In addition to the loud voice that Matt had, he also displayed a significant degree of
irrational behaviour when drinking…which we did often. After several bottles
of 'loud mouth', he wanted to do daredevil stupid things like trying to pick
fights with local constables. Of course, once he got something started, he would
call his buddy, Big Don, in to help. "Yeah, you've had it now! Big Don is gonna
kick your ass!"

So I learned tact through Matt. "No, officer. I do not desire any trouble and
I apologise humbly for my inebriated friend. Honestly, I have never seen him
like this before," I lied on several occasions. Due to his behaviour, Matt earned
the nickname 'Antichrist' from his fellow pilots. I don't have enough space here
to relate even half of my experiences with Matt, but I think you might enjoy
one or two.

Matt and I had flown missions together during the first night and day of Operation Just Cause – the successful invasion of Panama. Having done the invasion
thing and returned home to a 'hero's welcome' that we didn't really deserve,
Matt and I were on our way back to Panama. With the offensive operations over,
we were on the way to play our part in Operation Promote Liberty – the 'nation
building' phase.

We had been given a stack of travellers' cheques to spend during the open-
ended assignment, but since we'd be living on an air force base down there, we
would have little need for money. Accordingly, we had all decided to try and
spend all of it the night before we left. We were in Charleston, South Carolina,
waiting for a ride on a C-5 Galaxy. Our scheduled departure at 0700 left us with
about thirteen glorious hours in that fun town. We started with dinner. We or-

dered several of the most expensive entrées, followed by dessert, then Irish coffees; and so it went. I managed 113 bucks on dinner alone, back when a dollar went a lot further than it does now. The Irish coffee started the drinking phase, and began what seemed like an endless stream of Long Island iced teas, B–52s and a host of other mixed drinks. From what I can remember, we went through most of our cash, but nobody won our imaginary game of seeing who could spend it all in one night.

Matt, of course, turned into the Antichrist at about drink number three or four and went crazy. He was obnoxious and definitely headed for trouble so I left him and struck out on my own. Eventually, I decided to get some sleep a few hours later; we were to report to the front desk at 0500 and I figured two hours ought to do it. Hey, I was young back then and could get away with such antics.

I fell asleep almost immediately but woke soon afterwards when the Antichrist showed up with some locals in tow. I kicked them out but they kept coming back, wanting to party. Somehow I fell asleep again but only for a short time. When I awoke to the alarm, I showered and got ready to leave. Matt, with whom I shared a room, had passed out and was mysteriously missing his clothes. I don't know how he got that way; it was not my business. I tried repeatedly to get him up, but he was out cold. I was tired of always having to 'police him up', so I just left him there. However, just before leaving the room, I picked up a half melted bucket of ice cubes and poured it over him. He screamed like a school girl and started cursing, so I walked out; I was done with it.

Some minutes later, as I sat on the bus, a captain asked me, "Hey, Big Don, where's Matt?" "Asleep in the room," I responded flatly, knowing what was coming next. "You left him there? You never leave your wingman! What were you thinking?"

I wasn't thinking, of course. My head was spinning, and I was aching and starting to feel the effects of a big hangover. "Well, go get him!"

"Yes, Sir." And I hopped off the bus. When I opened the door, nothing had changed except that Matt had thrown up all over himself. Disgusted, I threw a sheet over him, quickly rolled him up in it like a human burrito and threw the unpleasant bundle over my shoulder. With Matt flailing and cursing all the way, I carried him down to the bus and dropped him onto the seat, naked as a jaybird, wrapped up in a stinky white sheet and cursing like a sailor, much to everyone else's amusement. I had done well in the eyes of my fellow drunken aviators and we left. Matt soon passed out, of course, so he ended up arriving in Panama in about the same condition. I checked him in like a piece of baggage, depositing him in plain view for everyone to inspect and ridicule, while I busied myself collecting my bags. That was Matt, the Antichrist, a guy who we learned to love over the years.

Then there was 'Stretch', the only guy who was taller than me. Mitch, as 'Stretch's' parents had named him, stood an impressive six-feet five-inches tall, and was also assigned to the smallish OH-58. Both fresh out of flight school, he and I were assigned to the same aviation unit in West Germany, back when that nation still used to have an East and a West. We were totally wet behind the ears and hardly knew our middle names, let alone anything of value about flying.

We found ourselves part of the Aeroscout Platoon of A-Company, Third Aviation Battalion, Combat in the 3rd Infantry Division. Our platoon comprised ten Kiowas and enough pilots to man about half of them. It was a cool place with a tremendous leader: Captain Coleman. He knew the value of trust and, from day one, assigned us our own ships. I became the proud owner of aircraft number 15572. Mine was different from the rest. The other nine were painted the standard dark green colour of the day, but mine had a bright yellow tail boom, landing gear, vertical stabiliser, main and tail rotor, and some antennas. I was told it had been crashed recently and was nearing a return to service following a lengthy rebuild. During the next week, I watched patiently as it became more and more complete until, one day, it was finally finished. When I asked my crew chief if it was ready to fly, he replied that it was and it was only awaiting a test flight.

Stretch was standing with me at the time of the subsequent fateful discussion. "Test flight, huh? Well, great. How about after lunch?" The puzzled crew chief, whom I hardly knew, asked me if I was a test pilot. I thought about it. During leave recently, I had just rebuilt a small block Chevy engine. Surely I knew all about maintenance! "Sure, I know a bunch about maintenance."

With the crew chief's somewhat confused acceptance, we reached an agreement for me and Stretch to fly the rebuilt machine. Wow! Finally we were going to go flying.

Lunch came and went, and Stretch and I hooked up the ground-handling wheels as we had seen the crew chiefs do a few times in the past couple of days. I grabbed the tail boom and the three of us pushed the bird out onto the apron. Stretch and I busied ourselves with an extra long pre-flight, then climbed in and put our helmets on. Over near the hangar, we noticed Mr. Furr, with a coffee mug clutched in his hand, watching us as we called "Clear" and hit the start button. The Allison whined to life and the start fuel ignited with its customary 'whomp'. As the start sequence continued and the ship spun up to a shaky ground idle, Stretch and I felt on top of the world; we were helping out with something important – and all under the watchful gaze of the most senior pilot in the battalion.

Mr. Furr was feared by all. He seldom talked to anyone, except to say "No!" or blast them out of his office in fits of rage that resembled blasts from a 20-mm Vulcan cannon. He had been in Vietnam, flown Chinooks, and was now in the twilight of a career that had spanned almost thirty years. Despite that, here he was, taking time out to notice we two fledgling pilots.

Stretch and I talked as we continued the run up. Finally, with our checklist complete and the machine running at 100 percent, we ran out of ideas. "What now?" we asked each other; I had no idea. "Why don't we just pick it up into a hover and kick the pedals around some?" Well, since they had just changed the tail rotor, main rotor, transmissions and engine, I figured it would be a good idea to make sure nothing would break off. And so that is exactly what we did. The ship responded with big changes to the rotor rpm as we jammed in right then left pedal.

All the while, Mr. Furr watched us – poker-faced and with his coffee cup at the ninety. Had we not been doing our 'test flight', he would have probably been sitting at his desk in the battalion maintenance office reloading rifle am-munition…his personal hobby. He was the senior army test pilot – not only in our battalion, but also, I believe, in all of Europe. He was *the* man. And lucky us; we had his undivided attention.

The crew chief was looking at us as if we were Martian invaders, but what did he know about pilot stuff? Anyhow, it all held together, so I took my turn going up and down, and doing 360 degree pedal turns. Eventually satisfied, we landed and allowed the engine to idle for two minutes to cool down. Then, clos-ing the throttle, we opened the door, took off our helmets and sat back like Tom Cruise fresh from a hop at Top Gun school.

The crew chief came up and asked me what the hell that had been. "A test flight," I told him. "What do you think?" We got out, tied the blades down, collected our stuff, then started walking deliberately towards Mr. Furr, who still stood in the same pose he had struck when we first started. I didn't know whether to salute, say hello or what, but I never got the chance.

"Boys, come over here," he demanded. "What was that just now; what did you just do?"

"Sir, 572 needed a test flight so we did it." Damn, that poker face of his was good!

"Test flight, huh? Are you two test pilots, or something?"

"Well, sir, I know something about maintenance and…"

I never got to finish. Mr. Furr exploded like a ten-kiloton nuclear blast.

"What the hell was that? Who the hell do you think you are? You two are finished. I'll have you both drawn and quartered! If you survive, you're through in the army! I'll have you court-martialled! That's the dumbest thing I have ever seen…" and so on and so on.

Scores of eyes watched us from behind Hueys, dumpsters, cars and other assorted bits of cover as Stretch and I stood at attention for a humiliating dressing down. We were immediately famous (or, rather, infamous); the two biggest boneheads the battalion had ever seen, apparently. I immediately remembered some advice my father had given me. A former military aviator himself, he once told me, "Son, don't ever do anything to make yourself famous." Now, here I was – at the start of only my second week since becoming an officer – and I was already 'famous'.

While, somewhat surprisingly, no nickname ever came out of that, Stretch and I served as the butt end of about half a million jokes for quite some time afterwards. Yep, we paid dearly. I learned there was such a thing as a 'pilot-in-command' – which I was not – and a 'maintenance test pilot' – which I also was not. Thereafter, until nearly the day I left, some years later, Mr. Furr always introduced me as: "that dumb-ass who test-flew a helicopter his first week in aviation."

So, my friends, a word to the wise: if you are contemplating doing something you might think of as an 'adventure', remember, you might end up either basking in the limelight – or wilting under the scrutiny of a courtroom-like drama with a bunch of clerks passing judgment over your actions and deciding your fate. So be careful. Or, on the other hand, just charge ahead with reckless abandon, take whatever comes your way and have a great time doing it. As for me? Well, I think you already know which fork in the road I took!

Chapter 17

DISTANT
THUNDER

Pre-flight is invariably a noisy time, even though they usually take place in the very early morning. The world around me is already well into the day's activities by the time I start to peer through my still sleepy eyes at the myriad of parts that comprise my flying machine.

However, one morning, amid all the noise of jets taking off and landing and helicopters hovering around on the ramp, there were some brief periods of relative quiet. It was during one of those short oases of calm that I heard it – far away, but unmistakable. First came the 'boom, boom, boom' of big guns firing. Then, after some time, the familiar 'crump, crump, crump' of those deadly 105s or larger 155s finding their mark. Once heard, these sounds are never forgotten, Outgoing or incoming artillery has a very distinctive sound indeed, and it is all too familiar.

Familiar to me, at least. I suspect the average family living in 'who-knows-where-ville' probably has no idea what real artillery sounds like.

"Mummy, what's that?"

"Oh, that's the 155s firing, dear." Perhaps Dad correcting: "No, actually, those are 105s – listen to the slightly higher pitch of the report."

No. I'll bet that conversation never happens at all, which is a good thing. Most people live in such opulent peace that a sound like that would probably strike panic into their hearts and overload the local phone system with emergency calls. But to some, a chosen few, it is just another 'normal' sound in a very different sort of everyday life.

I began thinking back to the times when I had heard similar sounds before; the sounds of the machines of war. My first real exposure to the big guns was probably when I first went to Grafenwöhr, Germany, as a young army sergeant. 'Graf', as we all called it, was, and remains, the site of a large armour training base for both the US and German armies where the guns hammer away at the German countryside 24/7 in endless training.

My first trip to Graf was in the turret of a trusty M-60A1 tank in which I served as the commander's gunner. A buck sergeant at the time, I had not yet won my slot to flight school and was still an enlisted soldier. I remember parking behind some very large eight-inch tracked artillery pieces as they fired. Eight inches does not refer to the length of the shell but the diameter of the bore of the cannon – a full eight inches across. (203 mm for the metrically-inclined readership.) Its shells – which it hurled some considerable distance – weighed so much that they were not easily handled and had to be pushed around on a kind of sled device. If you were looking at just the right spot when those guns fired, you could actually see the huge projectiles leave the tubes on their way up and outbound.

That M-60 tank was not to be trifled with either. It mounted a deadly 105-mm gun (4.13-inches in English-speak). Tanks' guns are not artillery, but rather, direct firing weapons, meaning that they fire in a direct line (like a rifle) rather than 'lobbing' their projectiles like big cannons. Our mission at the time was to train to become proficient at dispatching Russian tanks, a job that I eagerly (and foolishly) looked forward to. We were pretty good at our craft and could easily hit a tank-sized target every three to four seconds, even if on the move. This was back in the days before all the electronics that make the modern tank crewman an espresso while simultaneously engaging a hoard of enemy armoured vehicles!

Another 'once heard, never forgotten' sound is the 'brrrrrrr' of the Dillon or General Electric mini guns; that sound is eternally burned into my memory. Mini guns turn any aerial platform upon which they are mounted into hellish killing machines and are nothing short of terrifying to those on the receiving end.

Shortly after I was recruited to join the army's special operations aviation, I remember watching a pair of 'Little Birds' (Hughes OH-6 Cayuse) working out on the range at Fort Campbell, Kentucky. The Little Birds were flying in towards their target, 'bumping' up briefly and then pushing over. At the point where their noses aligned with the target, the distinctive long 'brrrrrrr' sound of the mini guns' firing began. The aircraft left smoke trails from the many hundreds of rounds being consumed and showered brass cases and steel links behind them. The target was momentarily 'alive' with a shower of sparks and ricochets; so many, in fact, that the effect was like a vertical wall of sparks such as one would see when welding steel. That sound creeps into one's inner being and, once there, is always recognisable.

For many years now, I have known the sound of the mini gun; at times, pairs of them pouring their streams of fire outwards from where I sat. Let me tell you, even sitting behind one, it is quite something when one of those guns goes off. For a pilot, sitting in front of one and slightly off to one side while it is firing, feels like an out of body experience. It is as if someone has poked a tiny hole into the very gates of hell and its contents are spraying through that hole at supersonic speeds. Now imagine that the hole is directly behind you and you will start to get the picture.

When you first hear the sound of a mini gun up close, your every instinct is to get away from it – as far away and as quickly as possible. However, I have bumped the helicopter so many times myself in a heavy gun bird with two willing Dillons in the back ready to digest 9,000 rounds of ammo that I have grown accustomed to the sound. I have heard those guns go 'hot' on so many occasions that I can scarcely remember specific moments. Now, to me, (as they say in the movies) it has become 'the sound of freedom'.

The sound of the way-too-big 30-mm Gatling gun fitted to the rather blunt nose of the A-10 'Warthog' (a similar 'brrrrr' but lower pitched than that of the mini gun) is another instantly recognisable auditory experience that I first encountered in Germany. At the time, the A-10 was an important but not yet battle-tested member of the combined arms team of aerial and ground warriors. These solid attack aircraft were working on a range at Hohenfels at the same time as my tank platoon. During a 'movement to contact' (where we were moving cautiously down a range while silhouettes of T-62 Russian tanks began to pop up), the Warthogs arrived to save the day. Until this point, as a young twenty-something sergeant, I had thought I was virtually invincible inside the lumbering steel hulk of my modern battle tank. The work of the A-10s was spectacular to see and hear.

While the targets kept popping up, we were fighting our platoon in two groups. The heavy section had over watch with three tanks, while the two most forward tanks, the light section, advanced carefully. In theory, it was the job of the light section to get a fight going, while the heavy section was supposed to provide overwhelming firepower to destroy anything opposing us.

However, as any soldier with a few more years' experience (and cynicism) would point out, one of the principles of war is that 'no plan remains intact after contact'. From my years of practical application of many well thought out plans, I can confirm that this cynical 'principle' is pretty much a true statement.

We were moving steadily down the range – picking through our mighty targets of plywood one by one and drilling them with 105-mm holes – when a pair of A-10s turned up and stole the show. They came ripping in just above the treetops, pulled up steeply, rolled inverted, pulled their noses up (down) and waxed the whole darned stinking range. They killed everything in about three milliseconds. The pilot of the second aircraft did a double tap. After the inverted bump, he rolled upright and immediately shot a cluster of tanks then snapped off hard to the right. In the middle of the turn, he turned back into another bump, shot another group of tanks – while upside down – and then split off to my left. Whoa! What the hell was that? Our entire company of tankers was thinking the same things: (1) Did we really just see that? (2) We are out of work, and (3) Do the Ruskies have anything like that to shoot at us with?

And yet, oddly enough, the A-10 is not a favourite of the US Air Force. I believe it must be some quirky fraternity thing, because, in my opinion, anyone who loves to fly a warplane and kill stuff should be kicking down doors to fly that beast. Of course, the A-10 is a close-air-support aircraft, which means it lives near the dirty, army-infested ground and any self-righteous true fighter pilot lives for only one thing: to kill another fighter. A real fighter pilot likes to take off from his or her base and rocket up toward MiG Alley for an afternoon shoot-fest, then back to base for steak and a couple of whiskey sours at the 'O' club (all of you zoomies out there reading this know it's true). But for me, a muddy-boot army soldier, the A-10 reigns supreme.

The A-10 came into its own in the blackened desert north of Saudi Arabia during Desert Storm. Those Warthogs accounted for many times their weight in enemy casualties. From the base I flew out of initially (KKMC or King Khalid Military City), the air force's A-10s sortied relentlessly. Their young pilots would even skip lunch in order to sortie faster and destroy more stuff before nightfall. Even then, they did not stop flying. I can't begin to imagine the terror the Iraqi soldiers must have felt when they heard the sound of the Warthog's General Electric CF-34 turbofans or, worse still, its terrible GAU-8 cannon. Believe me, there are many Iraqis alive today who will immediately wake from a dead sleep at the sound of that gun firing.

It affects me the same way. Just the other day, after an exhausting ten hours or so in the cockpit, followed by a few more hours of answering stupid emails from a bunch of clerks in the States, I was enjoying a deep, deep sleep. All at once, I was awake and sitting upright – as were two of the three other pilots with whom I shared the room. Reaction number one: awaken. Reaction number two: determine the location. Before I was even fully awake, my senses had my head turned toward the left. Then, an instant later, another 'BRRRRRR'! It was the unmistakable sound of an A-10 firing a burst.

As reason slowly overtook startled reaction, I remembered we were only a couple of miles from the Tarnak range complex at Kandahar, Afghanistan. "Sounds like an A-10," I said in the darkness. Pat, directly opposite me, (who should have been asleep) answered immediately "Yeah, an A-10," while Tim made the comment that it was "probably over at Tarnak, test firing." I chuckled and noted that all three of us had had exactly the same reaction. Meanwhile, Dave continued to snore.

Then there are the other sounds – the ones you never get used to completely. The worst, of course, is incoming mortar, artillery or rocket fire. The most common of these for us in Afghanistan are the 107-mm Russian rockets. The first sound you hear is the 'BOOOOM' when they explode. The next thing you hear is the whelping 'giant voice' alarm and a voice shouting: "Rocket attack, rocket attack!"

Apart from the incoming stuff that can actually kill you, the most frightening thing you'll ever hear is the good guys shooting big rockets outbound. How many of you think an outgoing rocket sounds like the Space Shuttle being fired into orbit? If you raised your hand, that's a good thing – because it shows that you live in a place where it never happens. If you didn't raise your hand, what did you hear? Was it television footage of a patriot during Desert Storm, or an 'Attackum' in Afghanistan or Iraq? I'm sure some artillery type is bristling right now at the way I butchered the Attackum name (it's actually ATACMS – army tactical missile system) but hey, I'm just an aviator of obvious low breeding and poor education; a product of, please forgive me, the lowly army.

Well, here's a news flash: those ATACMS do not sound anything like the Space Shuttle being launched. They sound like volcanoes, the ones that formed the earth, all exploding at once. The first time I ever heard one, I'd have to say it nearly startled me to death. I was living in a different compound at the time, on the perimeter of the ever-growing Kandahar airfield. The access road to the base's guard towers ran right past our accommodation, which, as far as rockets were concerned, was either a bad or a good thing. My building sat some thirty feet away from a Hesco barrier wall, which was only around twenty feet away from the access road. Unknown to me, during the hours of darkness that night, the army had parked a tracked ATACMS launch vehicle adjacent to my room. Sometime in the late watches of the night when decent people ought to be sleeping – my world changed violently.

From a heavy sleep, in which I had been roaming around in dream land with my wife and children, I was blasted into reality by 150+ decibels of ear-ripping full-on 'afterburner jet noise'. My flimsy PVC plastic door, which was usually bright white, was now bright orange! My first thought was that a rocket had hit us and we were on fire. Then, a microsecond later, I thought perhaps one of the Dutch F-16s might have crashed into our compound immediately after take-off while still in afterburner. However, the fire-like orange light and the deafening sound started to decrease, as if whatever was causing it was getting further away. Obviously, if an F-16 had crashed on us, it couldn't have continued its take-off. So what the hell was going on?

Then, as the sound continued to diminish, there came a shower of something on our tin roof. It sounded as if someone had dropped a load of gravel from some height. Several seconds later, when the world hadn't ended, I hopped out of bed and cautiously opened the door. The orange light was now gone but as I looked down the hallway, I could see big Pete looking out the window in the door at his end of the building. Even in the pale light, I could see his big South African smile as he turned to look at me and said, "That was a big one!"

Big what? Meteor? Atomic bomb? What? Then someone more knowledgeable than me voiced that name that I will always remember: "Attackum." Immediately thereafter, thanks to Google and the internet, we all became Attackum-smart.

To look at those things and to actually experience one being fired is altogether different. Suffice it to say, you don't want to experience something like that – unless you're the type who needs to climb into the engine of a Boeing 757 during the take-off roll just to heighten the senses.

I could get into learning about the patriot sound, but it's little different from the Attackum. Even if you knew one was to be fired and you were given a countdown, you would still jump halfway out of your skin when it actually went off.

So, I guess, in retrospect, when I hear the 'boom, boom, boom…crump, crump, crump' of distant artillery, I guess it isn't really so bad after all. The fact that I know that sound (and a whole catalogue of other noises, and a dictionary of terms that are meaningless in everyday conversations back home) while many of you do not is also a good thing. It means that some dedicated, selfless people are doing a great job of keeping such sounds away from your ears. So if you get a chance, take a knee in some private place and pray to your God. Thank him for these people and for the fact that because of what they do, you do not know about such things.

Chapter 18

WILD
RIDE

Have you ever played the game 'There I was…?' It is a well-known drinking game that is (or was) commonly played in the backrooms of officers' clubs worldwide. It involves a story – or rather, a fantastic collection of lies – spun together by a host of pilots who are heavily under the influence of alcohol. It starts something like this:

"There I was," (the mandatory opening line), "inverted, in a flat spin, air medals dangling in my face," or something similar. Each successive liar adds his spice to the tale, "Number two was on fire," then, another: "Number one had just been hit by a goose," and so on, until the tale becomes too long or the number of liars is finally exhausted.

I believe that while each of us 'seasoned' aviators probably has a story or two of our own to tell, there is perhaps a limit to the number of tales of high adventure one can accumulate because, in the business of flying, you don't always get to survive an adventure. My Dad used to say it like this: "Son, in your life, you need to get yourself a few rocking chair stories." Then with a pause for effect and with a slight warning in his tone, he would say "But just a few!" That advice, coming from a guy who had had three planes shot out from under him and who used to drop high explosive bombs on Nazi Germany while Messerschmitts chewed up the formations, was both sobering and sound.

Reading my previous letters, you have already heard one or two of my 'rocking chair stories'. The other day, while thinking about some near misses I have had, an incident that happened to me one dark night came to mind. The good ones usually happen to you when you least expect them and when you are least prepared. I think of them as little pop quizzes about life. Earn an 'F' and you do not get to go on. A grade of 'C' will probably get you some extended hospital time and physical therapy, while an 'A' or a 'B' means you have been either extraordinarily lucky and/or delivered simultaneously by the Almighty himself.

I think it was a Friday evening. I say that because in the traffic pattern at Fort Campbell Army Airfield, there were scarcely any aircraft flying. I was giving a pilot his annual flight proficiency evaluation flight or check ride. All the other pilots were over at the officers' club telling 'there I was' stories. Unknown to me, I was about to live through one myself – but this one would be for real.

The evaluation was going very well. We flew around the traffic pattern and as I simulated shutting down one or other of the engines of our MH-47 special operations modified Chinook, Rick, the guy I was evaluating, performed the appropriate corrective actions. Rick was a recent addition to the spec-ops (special operations) community and was one of our maintenance test pilots. Basically, after we (the mission pilots) flew around and broke things, he and others like him spent long days and nights trying to fix the broken aircraft – while we told our stories, holding long-necked bottles at the ready.

I liked everything I had seen so far. We had done a variety of engine malfunctions and electrical problems, and I had even turned off the AFCS (advanced flight control system). The giant two-headed dipsy dumpster (Chinook) could not possibly fly without some computer constantly fixing its wandering attitude about 4,000 times a second and this is the job of the AFCS, which is a little jewel of a system. The Chinook's giant aft rotor has a nasty tendency to want to pass the front rotor in forward flight, and the wonderful gyros and gizmos in the AFCS computer immediately stop all that nonsense regardless of what the pilot might be doing. Pilots are unaware of what the AFCS does – until about three milliseconds after it is turned off in flight, whereupon the 100-foot long helicopter first tries to swap ends, then roll sideways, then pitch over and crash – all in about two seconds. Nevertheless, flying without AFCS was something I demanded that pilots were proficient at because in combat conditions, there is always a possibility of that valuable little computer being damaged. So we had to know how to fly the machine without the electronic stability. Most guys were not very good at it, and as an instructor pilot, it was my job to take over if the other guy lost control and provide instruction on how I did it.

Anyhow, Rick was better than most with AFCS-off flight, so we departed the traffic pattern for the low-level training area. Once there, we did a variety of terrain flight tasks including landing in a cool little confined area where there was a clearing in the trees barely larger than the aircraft. He didn't seem to be having any difficulty with that either, so I thought I'd finish the check ride with some instrument flight.

Flying at low altitude, which was less than fifty feet in this case, while wearing night vision goggles is a tricky proposition. It is a regime of flight where one needs complete trust in the guy doing the driving. If he screwed up on anything, the helicopter will probably be chopping firewood long before an instructor can jump on the controls and save the day, or night. We had to be able to fly around at low level with goggles in weather conditions where visibility was as low as half a mile – which isn't very much at all.

If one were to 'punch in' or suddenly lose sight of the ground, then there was a detailed procedure that had to be executed immediately to save one's bacon and get the aircraft out of harm's way. The steps were to announce "Inadvertent IMC" (meaning inadvertent instrument meteorological conditions or, simply, you're in the clouds). The next step was to level the wings (the term is also used in helicopters) and pull in climb power – basically, all the power the engines will give you – and commence an aggressive climb. You would then turn to avoid known obstacles and get on the 'guard' radio frequency to get air traffic control (ATC) involved to get help.

I initiated this scenario by holding my map in front of Rick's goggles while telling him, "I have a tower at twelve o'clock, 500 metres." Once again, he demonstrated the correct response. Rick said in an even tone, "I'm inadvertent IMC. Turning left to one eight zero, climbing to 3,000." Cool. The guy even knew the sector minimum altitude; he was obviously completely in control of the situation. I liked his decision to climb immediately to get away from those pesky oak trees below us, and his smooth execution of the climb.

The thing I liked about ending the check ride in such a way was that it was a less stressful mode of flying and a great transition from the nerve-racking emergencies to controlled flight in a radar-monitored environment where someone was talking to us. We levelled at 3,000 feet and I contacted Campbell Approach Control. "Good evening, Campbell. Army 'Triple Sticks' is a single Chinook, level at 3,000, heading one eight zero, approximately ten miles south of Clarksville. Requesting an instrument recovery to the airfield." (I called our Chinook 'Triple Sticks', because the aircraft's serial number was 24111, so instead of saying "one, one, one", we simply say triple sticks – it just sounds better.)

"Roger, Triple Sticks. Squawk three-two-one-four." Then, after we were identified:

"Army Triple Sticks, Campbell Approach has you radar contact fifteen miles south of the Clarksville VOR. State intentions." I looked at Rick, who said,

"Let's get an ILS (instrument landing system) approach."

"Campbell Approach, we would like an ILS to a full stop."

"Roger that, Triple Sticks. Turn left to zero two zero. This will be vectors to ILS runway two-two."

This was going very well indeed. In retrospect, it was a setup for what was about to happen. The crew in the back, a flight engineer and a crew chief, were practically asleep and I had relaxed completely. In just a few more minutes, we would be on the ground, and could put this old bird to sleep for the night and, hopefully, get some sleep ourselves.

We followed the ATC vectors until we eventually intercepted the inbound course about thirteen miles from the runway. "Army triple sticks, I show you established on ILS two-two. Contact the tower on frequency one two six point four. Have a good night."

Rick continued to fly so I dialled in the tower frequency. "Good evening, Tower. Triple Sticks is with you, ILS inbound."

"Roger that, Triple Sticks. You are cleared to land runway two-two."

I noticed the glide slope appear on the HSI (horizontal situation indicator instrument). As it passed through the centre lubber line, Rick reduced power and we began our descent. This dude was flying like an airline pilot and finishing a great night with a professional job on the last approach. Had I been awarding a numerical grade for this ride, it would have been in the high nineties.

At five miles, he had all the wind corrections and power figured out, and the aircraft descended smoothly as if locked into that electronic cross we were flying down. As we drew ever closer to the ground, I announced, "500 above", signalling that he was 500 feet above the decision height – the point at which he would have to decide either to continue to a landing or go around. "200 above", I voiced as we descended. Then, "100 above", Rick's night vision goggles were turned off and still flipped down. I had turned them off earlier to prevent him from looking outside. Their being switched off also provided a great 'hood' that confined his visual field of view to just the instrument panel.

"You're at decision height," I advised him. "Great job. Take over visually and land abeam taxiway three." Taxiway three led straight to our parking spot and I was done messing around for the night. As Rick tilted his head back and pulled in power to arrest our descent, I noticed the flight engineer standing in the companionway just behind us. Suddenly, just as Rick increased power, both engines went wide open. With no warning at all, the dammed things just went to full power.

In those days, the Chinook had two very powerful Lycoming L-712 engines that produced 4,500 horsepower each. They were so powerful that the aircraft could maintain cruise flight at maximum gross weight on just one engine. Now, suddenly and violently, both engines had a malfunction called a 'high side', meaning that the governors had failed and both simply went wide open.

With so much power being generated, the rotor system started to over-speed rapidly. The normal operation range for the rotor RPM was from ninety-seven percent to 101 percent. I was looking at a rotor speed approaching 110 percent. The emergency procedure calls for the pilot to immediately pull an armload of power to load the engine that is high siding. Theoretically, this *should* reduce the rotor RPM back to within controllable limits immediately. Rick was doing exactly that, but the lightly loaded Chinook was about to spin the rotor blades right off the top of the helicopter. In all my days, I had never seen, or even heard of, two engines high-siding at the same time; it had never happened before. But both torque needles (which indicate individual engine power output) were joined up at around eighty percent meaning both engines were over-speeding simultaneously. I couldn't believe it was happening, so I asked – or, more correctly, yelled – "What's happening?" Rick yelled back, "High side. High side. Both engines."

OK. We were screwed! There wasn't an emergency procedure for this, so I improvised. I announced "I have the controls. Take 'one' to ground." The only thing I could think to do was to pull number one to idle, so that we could focus on dealing with just engine number two. We were climbing very quickly. It had only been seconds and we were already climbing through 1,000 feet and going up at more than 3,000 feet a minute. I squeezed the transmit switch: "Tower, Triple Sticks is declaring an emergency."

They must have known something was out of the norm because they quickly started inquiring about our fuel state, personnel on board and so forth. "No time, Tower. Clear the runway. I have two runaway engines!" I heard something about crash rescue rolling and something else, but I was too busy trying to fly the thing to worry.

As soon as Rick pulled number one to ground (an idle position with the engine control lever), the rotor RPM responded immediately and came back down. As it reduced through about 100 percent I decreased power and we stopped climbing. The runway was still below me so I lowered the thrust control and we began descending. At around a 1,000 feet, I added a little power to slow the descent. Without warning, the rotor blades began slowing uncontrollably. The spinning of the rotor blades is all that keeps a helicopter in the air. The atmosphere naturally rejects the helicopter and only the constant thrashing of the blades keeps the things aloft. Some might argue about aerodynamics or some silly physics, but it's simply not true; it's all just magic, smoke and mirrors.

I told Rick to give me more power but the blades continued to slow. I bottomed the thrust and, in an instant, that Chinook was in a full-blown autorotation. There was no time left. The ground – thankfully, a runway – was coming up fast. As we passed through 200 feet, we were descending at 2,500 feet per minute. I eased the nose up to start the flare; 100 feet, then fifty. I flared hard and pulled in all my remaining power.

The aft wheels slammed into the runway roughly but held. I pulled the nose up twenty degrees and tried to hold it there. I shot a glance inside and saw the engine tachometers decreasing below thirty-five percent. Idle was sixty-two percent, so obviously, both engines had failed at some point. The blades continued to slow. We were going like a bat out of hell on two wheels and I had to get this thing slowed down. Then the next hammer blow hit us. The rotors were no longer going around fast enough to drive the generators, so they dropped offline, giving us a total electrical failure.

Even though I was an instructor pilot, I didn't know that the swivel-locks on the aft wheels unlocked when there wasn't any electrical power (swivel-locks keep the wheels locked fore and aft, and disengage to allow steering the aircraft while taxiing). This came as a huge surprise because suddenly, the wallowing giant started fishtailing wildly from side to side. We went almost completely sideways while still rolling forwards until, finally, the rotor blades slowed so much that I couldn't hold the nose up any longer. We slid sideways and the front came down heavily. All I could think of was that we were about to roll over, so I yelled: "Duck!"

Something reminded me of being in a skidding car; you always turn in the direction of the skid. The nose was sliding around to the left, so I leaned forward and pulled the cyclic into my gut and to the left. I felt the rotor blades beating heavily on their droop stops above my head, seemingly pounding poor Triple Sticks to pieces. For what seemed like an eternity, we skidded around and around. I smashed the brakes with my size twelves and we slid off the runway going backwards.

Then, about as fast as it had started, the helicopter stopped. There was no sound or movement. I sat up, not believing we hadn't rolled over or caught fire or something. We had touched down about midfield on a runway that was 11,000 feet long, and we were sitting in the grass perhaps 2,000 feet from the end, pointing back more than 180 degrees from the way we had come, and the blades had stopped completely. For a long second, we all just sat there looking around. Then the crew chief said, "Sir, we're smoking, we're smoking." Indeed, smoke was coming up from the ruined tyres and brakes, and both engines were smoking out of each end. It was pretty dark outside but we could see it anyway.

I ordered everyone out and instructed them to assemble 100 feet off the nose.

I heard the crewmembers running down the ramp. Rick had a crazy look on his face. I motioned out with my thumb and he jumped out of the aircraft in about three steps. I got up and looked down the large cargo hold with my flashlight. There was no one left; it was clear. Time to 'didi-mau' myself and leave the wreck to its fate. I gave about a half second's thought to fighting the fires but decided I'd rather watch the helicopter burn after what it had just tried to do to all of us and I, too, jumped off.

I met the guys where we had briefed, about a 100 feet in front of the nose of the Chinook. We all watched as the crash rescue vehicles came screaming down a taxiway close to us. Then, incredibly, they turned away from us and went racing to the other end of the runway! Remember, it was very dark and, on a military airfield, lights are kept at a minimum. We all broke out in hysterical laughter as our 'saviours' drove away at breakneck speed.

Glancing back at the bird, it didn't seem to be on fire anywhere, despite the smoke, so I walked back over to it and stared at the immense black form. Tonight had been a date with destiny for all of us. The grim reaper had been in attendance, no doubt, but on this night, through some crazy mix of luck, correct guesses – choosing door number two instead of number one – and so forth, we had cheated his clutches. We would live to fly again. So, too, would this aircraft, although only after it had received two new engines, six tyres, four brakes and a bunch of other parts.

So goes my very real 'There I was' story. To tell it engenders all the emotions one experiences in danger and combat. The emotions run back and forth from fear, to confusion, to anger and, finally, to satisfaction and elation – elation at knowing one escaped…but just barely. I have written before about that feeling one gets upon narrowly escaping death. You have to experience it to understand it (but I do not necessarily recommend that you do so) and I cannot begin to describe it. It brings you to a place where you mentally crest a small rise and start down the other side where the downhill slide is irreversible. A change takes place in your very soul. You can never be quite the same again. You have become a veteran of sorts, and you start to see yourself as very mortal, very lucky, and very, very blessed.

Chapter 19

MISSIONS

We were cruising along at 135 indicated. I had Band on the Run (the old Paul McCartney/Wings song) stuck in my head and was singing it loudly. The big bird, our cargo ship, was close behind. I could feel the steady 'thump, thump, thump' of those big blades beating the air into submission somewhere behind us. The outside temperature was a very 'pleasant' nine degrees Celsius but the windshields and the well-sealed doors were keeping everything toasty warm inside my Italian 'sports car' of a helicopter. With my singing breaking into the intercom through the 'vox' every once in awhile, I'm sure Kaz thought I was a little off my rocker that morning, but who cared? "Band on the run… Band on the run"…I didn't know too many of the rest of the lyrics, but the melody was rocking away in my head. Earlier, before we launched, Gerry had been banging away playing the song on Guitar Hero and I had made the mistake of listening to him play. Now the thing was stuck in my head for the day.

"What a day!" I announced loudly over the intercom. "Another day in the ROA!" (Republic of Afghanistan.) I intentionally left out the word Islamic because it just doesn't rhyme as well; so for me, it's just ROA. What a day, indeed. We had the wind at our back, and someone had given us the keys to a 15,000,000 dollar helicopter with a tank full of gas, and a credit card. Now just how bad could that be?

How bad *could* it be? Well, several thousand feet below our comfortable cockpit was a world turned on its very end. The nearby road was scarred every couple of hundred metres with burned blotches where men had met their fates from the blasts of RPGs or IEDs. If we were to fly much lower than we were, it would place us within the engagement range of small-arms fire. In the airspace above and all around us were fighters with their wings laden with bombs. On any given day, some of those bombs would find their mark after falling several miles through the atmosphere. In other places in the sky, tankers orbited refuelling various aircraft and, at lower altitudes, other helicopters made their way methodically along to various destinations. At the end of some of those days, not all of those helicopters would taxi back into their revetments or parking spots, and men with long faces would sit in a noisy mess hall and stare into their cups of coffee, their thoughts far, far away.

The US Army calls the area here 'battle-space', a term which describes not only the surface of the planet but all the cubic miles of sky which lie above it. All of that space is carefully managed, and being able to move about within it at any time is a matter of careful planning and control. Just as choreographers work out every step in complicated stage productions, so do the controllers manage some parts of their battle-space. They orchestrate all the moving parts of this air-land battle, and somehow keep it safer and moving along. Not only do they manage aircraft, but also long pointy mindless projectiles that originate in fiery births from the muzzles of cannons to live short, arching lives before finally becoming fire themselves. We have an expression here: 'Big sky; little bullet' to describe flying in the proximity of artillery. I don't know if any aircraft have accidentally been hit by flying six-inch shells but the potential is definitely there.

For combat pilots, it has become a matter of routine to work with this system in lieu of more traditional air traffic controllers. The language spoken between the various controlling agencies probably sounds like some secret code (which I guess it is, in a way) to anyone who hasn't flown in this world.

Oh, by the way, we do 'live' in this world, we don't just work or fight in it. It becomes so pervasive and overwhelming that it actually becomes your world. There is no getting away from the hassle, hustle and bustle of a fast-paced military lifestyle. Except, perhaps – just occasionally – for pilots. We get to have little moments of escape every once in a while and, on this day, I was having mine. Sure it was at Kaz's expense; this day, he was the flight lead with all the attendant responsibility and workload while I was flying as his co-pilot. For me, it was 'mental vacation' time. Let him worry about all that navigation, fuel management and radio call business.

I was working out the lyrics for Band on the Run as we flew through the rugged mountains. Yesterday, I had been the flight lead and he had been co-pilot, and the cards had been reversed. Of course, in truth, the co-pilot can never get a complete mental vacation – he still has to look out for birds, unmanned aerial vehicles, other helos and occasional tracer rounds – but you get the picture.

Kaz is a great guy to fly with. With a thick Jersey accent and a short temper, there is never a dull moment. Take some time to get to know him and, in short order, you can find that big red button, which, I have discovered, is fun to push occasionally. Especially because he talks with his hands, for added entertainment. I like to push that button while he's flying and watch things get downright amusing. The man can't talk without moving his arms – well, not properly, anyway. But he sure can complain; he ranks right up there with the very best of them. If the day is a seven-hour one, it's too long. If it's a two-hour one, it's a waste of time. If lead is doing 120, we're too slow. If we're doing 140, the helicopter is too rough. I just love it. I keep trying to guess what might piss him off next or at any particular time, but honestly, I can't. He's an American original. Like everyone else here, I just love the guy. I love to hear the bitching and look forward to future complaining with eager anticipation. Call me weird, but it sure is fun.

Recently, the war seems to have got much worse for both sides. Everyone is suffering more than I can remember happening in the past. With ever-increasing numbers of soldiers pouring into the battle space, it is only natural that there is an increasing amount of contact with the enemy or NCF (non-coalition forces) as they have become known. There are so many different groups jumping into the fray here against the West that a single term was needed to describe the guys who shoot at us for a living.

With all the forces out there poking around in the bush, the need to re-supply them has increased proportionally. The helicopter has become the workhorse of the theatre, and pilots and machines are getting a real workout. I remember my comfortable days driving a jet around the atmosphere. Even though I flew an average of eighty-five hours a month for years, it was nothing like flying helicopters. Nowadays, eighty a month would be a vacation and a nice dream. No sir, we routinely knock out between 100-200 hours a month, every month. Frankly, I am amazed at the reliability of the machines. Almost daily, I log seven to nine hours, with only one start and ten to twelve sorties. Just yesterday, we did seventeen sorties, logging nine-and-a-half hours.

Without getting into the tactics, suffice it to say that certain phases of flight can be a real rollercoaster ride. We get no points for a smooth landing, it's always a slide in behind a barrier after a steep approach or 'S-ing' or some other technique. Take-offs are the same drill. Get speed fast, manoeuvre it like you stole it until you have enough speed, then it's aft cyclic and a firm pull on the 'up' lever to gain that all-important altitude. Combat pilots everywhere will agree: altitude and speed are life – and we like to live! It is not like that all the time, but if we go into a hairy LZ, then we bend that thing around until we're safely back at altitude.

Another great feature (not) of expanding war zones is the slow creep of influence from the 'clerks'. I believe my earlier writings might have mentioned these office dwellers occasionally. Some of them are great people, but others are warrior wannabe types. The latter are downright stupid and very difficult to deal with. Since they have only an academic understanding of what combat is like, they gravitate toward that understanding. As they are not actually participating in the fight stuff, they feel like they need to compensate (over-compensate) for not having paid their dues facing the wolf.

But as any field soldier knows, the clerks' text books belong in classrooms and are only useful for providing information about things like the specific weight of something you are going to carry. When it comes to tactics, it is a different story. All the mountains of experience of Vietnam, the Gulf and who knows where else doesn't equal an anthill of useful information in relation to 'the 'Stan'. Here, if you want to know what is going on, ask that dirty sergeant over there or strike up a conversation with those warrant officers in the corner of the chow hall. Those guys with their soiled uniforms and stained patches will give you the real story. They have learned from the school of hard knocks and they come into their own out there on the battlefield. The better they become out there, the further apart they become from the clerks that live 'inside the wire'.

A great example of the lack of understanding the clerks have for the combat crews is the speed limit of twenty kilometres per hour on our base. That's twelve American miles per hour. Vehicles do not easily travel that slowly. In order to do so, they tend to remain in low gear, which causes the engine to run at a faster speed, thereby generating heat. Heat which (in what is the hottest place on the planet sometimes) cannot be dissipated because at twelve miles per hour, there is NO airflow! To add insult to injury, the military police hang out around the flight line access roads with radar guns looking for 'speeders'. Unbelievable. They have nothing better to do than to issue traffic tickets to people 'speeding' along at twenty-five kilometres per hour.

Now picture a smallish SUV driving along the dusty perimeter road – 'hurtling' along at some twenty-two kilometres per hour. The three soldiers inside are aeroscout pilots who have just finished flying. They still have loaded assault rifles and pistols with them, which they might have used a few hours earlier. The reason there are only three of them and not four is because the fourth is in hospital – still in surgery – with a bullet in his abdomen, which came up through his hip. When that vehicle goes through the radar trap and is stopped, how much cooperation do you think the MP is going to get from those guys? Do you think the MP might possibly be in mortal danger himself?

We have to deal with the clerks every day, but like the guys in the SUV, while we also live on base, we work outside the wire. My mind often stays outside the wire, and sometimes, my ability to accommodate the clerks and their little American world inside it is a bit limited.

My first memorable meeting with a clerk came after a long (and eventful) night during Desert Storm. I had been up for so many hours that I felt too tired to sleep. My head was buzzing from flying all night long. Walking back to my quarters in the safety of my base, I was wearing only my dirty flight suit, which was devoid of rank and insignia; it had only coarsely drawn 'O+' symbols on the chest, back and arms. While going over the previous night's mission in my head, a piercing voice entered my consciousness.

Through a fog of exhaustion, a person came into focus in front me. He was a lieutenant-colonel, immaculately dressed from head to foot with all the latest battle stuff – all of which looked new and clean. I studied him from head to foot without really hearing what he was saying (we were supposed to wear all of our gear all the time – some sort of uniform policy – but hey, the war was fifty miles over my left shoulder).

Finally, I focussed enough to actually hear him. He was saying (screaming, by now), "Soldier, where's your Kevlar?" Meaning, where was my helmet? I thought for a second and said, "I don't know," and proceeded to walk straight through him, bumping him solidly as we met. When I turned, a few metres past him, to look back, he just stood there staring at me. A clerk, I thought, and walked back to my room.

Now you can just imagine the influence clerks might have with this expanding battle space. It takes air-conditioning-hogging rooms full of them to manage all this stuff. Hell, in their padded chairs inside their buildings of plywood or concrete, they account for the majority of Gatorade consumption in theatre. We, on the other hand, can't seem to get Gatorade or other sports-type drinks on the flight line; there is always a shortage. When working in heat or long hours, one needs to drink lots of fluids. Keeping hydrated and with a steady supply of electrolytes gives one the edge and fends off the ever-present headache waiting to overshadow a day, even one in which Band on the Run is beating out its rock and roll rhythm in my head.

I could go on and on about clerks, but I think I'll hold right here for now because I believe they deserve an article all of their own. Back to the battle space and mission. (I've strayed a bit, but it was fun, don't you think?)

Think of the aircrew, now, and what they have to deal with. Firstly, they are flying in Afghanistan, which is not the most hospitable place on the globe. Secondly, they are flying in helicopters, which have their own agenda. Remember that part of what they are always trying to do is to disintegrate suddenly and catastrophically. Then crews have to deal with about 300 radio calls an hour – and the intercom and radio systems in helicopters are not exactly what you find in the cushy cockpits of business jets. And, of course, they also have to do several things at the same time: look out for a flight of Apaches coming down orange route, contact hornet nest control on frequency 277.5, coordinate fuel at the upcoming stop and negotiate crossing the restricted airspace you are about to enter at 6,500. Whew, that takes longer to write than the time it takes to actually do it! So if you can juggle all those balls at once – and look cool while doing it, contact me right away – I have a job for you.

Looking at it that way, no mission is ever routine. The only routine parts are: always having to get up early, attend briefings, eat, pre-flight, jump in, crank up, shut down, call maintenance, and crank up again, taxi, take off and so forth. We might fly to the same destinations but never twice in exactly the same circumstances. Therefore, even the re-supply missions have their own unique set of variables to challenge us on any given day.

Like everything else in life, maybe it's better to just treat each flight as a unique challenge and see where it takes us. Most of us will end up sitting at a corner table in the chow hall tonight with our heads buzzing, enjoying some light conversation with fellow pilots. For some others, their tables will be silent and the food only picked over lightly. A small percentage will be there only in memory; those who have just had their last flights – their 'rendezvous with destiny'.

Chapter 20

AEROSCOUTS

The two young 'warrants' (warrant officers) caught my eye as they walked past my aircraft on their way towards their company area. They looked tired, very tired, and I noticed the green canvas boxes, which held their ANVIS night vision goggles, draped over their shoulders. Their faces were streaked with dirt or dust, and trails of tears led from the corners of their eyes – something that is common here, as our eyes are constantly irritated by all the dirt and dust in the air.

They had been out all night searching for a fight and, from the look of them, they had found one. I noticed how well the digital camouflage pattern of their ACU (army combat uniforms) blended in with the gravel they were walking on. The shorter warrant had his .223-caliber M4 carbine dangling from its short sling, which was attached to a loop near the top right shoulder of his vest. He was still wearing his heavy-armour vest while carrying his helmet bag, the night vision goggles, a map case and a scarf. The taller pilot was carrying his rifle in his right hand. His thumb was hooked around the ACOG (advanced combat optical gunsight) optic battle sight, and his fingers clutched at the magazine well, holding the weapon firmly. I noticed that a thirty-round magazine was still inserted. A full magazine, probably stuffed with the army's potent new seventy-seven-grain bullets.

Above me, the forward cowling of my machine was pushed forward to the limits as two mechanics busied themselves trying to repair my aircraft. A quick glance at my watch confirmed it; we were late again. We were supposed to have lifted off at 0750 and it was now nearing 0820. Earlier that chilly March morning, having cranked number two and waited for the oil temps to increase slightly,

I had been just about to spin it up to operating RPM when I noticed the master caution light was on and a 'No. 2 Servo' message was illuminated.

From the left seat, Brent (one of my pilots, who was an AW139 captain, an employee of Evergreen Aviation International) was looking at it also and we began to poke around. He flipped up the 'Hydraulics' page on his right screen, which gives a nice colour graphic of the system's status in real time – a cool feature built into sophisticated modern aircraft like the Agusta we were in. Sure enough, the right side hydraulic cylinders were all yellow in colour. Green is good, yellow not so much, and red is no good at all. The system indications showed a pressure of 204 bars and a temperature of thirty degrees Celsius. These were normal, so the problem was neither a lack of pressure, nor a high temperature condition – which meant it was probably some pesky little widget malfunctioning.

I never liked the fact that this European aircraft displayed metric data and not imperial. The units of measure had little meaning and I was not accustomed to them. A normal hydraulic pressure gage should read 3,000 PSI, not 204 Bar. What the heck is a 'bar' anyway? It's certainly not a unit of measure. A bar is a place you go to tell war stories! It didn't matter, of course – it wasn't green, so even for a backwoods dirt-floor Chinook guy, it meant we weren't going to turn any jet gas into noise anytime soon.

We were in a limbo status known to every pilot as the 'maintenance minute', which might last a minute…or it might last all day; one never knows which way the winds of fate are going to blow. For me, it wasn't looking good. We had already called the standby crew to spin up the larger Bell 214ST, which is something of a cross between a Mack truck and an old Huey. It is the largest two-blade-rotor helicopter on earth, and some believe if it were given a good enough anchor point, a Bell 214 could change the planet's celestial orbit. While I wouldn't go quite that far, I have certainly seen that truckster gobble up hundreds of boxes of mail. Last Christmas, I watched as enthusiastic soldiers stuffed boxes in every nook and cranny throughout the airframe. The back was full and there were boxes on the dash and under the seats; it was amazing. I thought of drawing a picture of it with boxes stuffed into the engine air inlets, a cargo net between the skids and a luggage rack on top. The 214 carries a lot of junk but it is not as fast as the AW139. I had woken this morning looking forward to two things – getting a good breakfast and then flying with another 139 where we could open our thoroughbreds up and let them run all day. Now all that was out the window, we were caught up in the great unknown of the 'maintenance minute'.

The mechanics were cursing and pulling on things. The work went on and on, and my hopes of flying up in the mountains today started to wane. Parts were flying and the pages of the aircraft's logbook looked like an exploded store catalogue. As the two warrants walked further away, someone dropped something heavy from above. I started as it smacked into the aluminium matting we were parked on. The taller warrant ducked in response to the bang and turned to look. He had been in the thick of it, all right. Once you get that 'set' in your nerves, it's a hard thing to lose.

I started thinking about the warrant officer's startled move. He was nearing the end of his one-year combat deployment with the 82nd Airborne Division. Known as the 'All Americans', the 82nd made its name in northern France in the early hours of D-Day. Their fearless men had borne their division into the culture of warriors in the US Army and countless since then had continued the tradition. The 82nd has served in every conflict our nation has been in-volved in since World War II and its men were known as the 'go to' guys in a tough fight. I had served with them many times during my military career, and now they were finishing their third combat deployment in Afghanistan.

That warrant would soon be back at Fort Bragg, North Carolina, and I won-dered if he had a family eagerly awaiting his return. His quick reactions told of a keen sense that had probably kept him alive during the past twelve months. I wondered if his reactions were going to help his reintegration into normal American society or hinder it. I didn't even know him, but I had a deep sense of respect for him and his friend. Soon, they would be replaced by the 101st Airborne Division (pronounced, 'one-oh-first') from Fort Campbell – another tough-as-leather fighting unit.

Watching that soldier made me think of others who reacted similarly to loud noises, flashes, quick movement and the like. The guy with the worst case of highly-strung nerves I knew was a friend and former commander, Russ Car-mody. I have mentioned him before and I respect him enormously, but I have to chuckle when I think about what I used to do to him. We all knew that loud noises like gunfire made him jumpy; everyone had witnessed it many times. One time, he was attending a graduation in the US and was standing in a group of other soldiers. When a gun fired as a part of the ceremony, he flung himself com-pletely prone on the ground and covered his head – at the speed of light. A per-son can't actually fall as fast as Russ did; he must have developed a form of powered flight downwards. Literally in the blink of an eye, that man went from standing to prone.

As a result, my fellow pilots goaded me into playing a series of jokes on the, then, major. All I had to do was create some loud noises, once with a big pot and once with a series of balloons, which I popped. All got the same reaction:

Russ would execute his 'powered down' manoeuvre and disappear under a desk or a bunk in a flash. He was a big guy and sometimes, I had to run to escape getting pounded by his flailing fists afterwards. He was a great guy, as well as a man of many nicknames. You already know that earning a nickname is a matter of considerable circumstance. Russ was variously called 'Rusty', 'Salamander Man' and 'Alonzo, the Human Torpedo', among others. Please, don't ask.

However, Russ wasn't the only one with extreme reactions. I remember the time I was driving my buddy's Z28 Chevrolet Camaro soon after returning from one conflict or another. I was cruising one of the back roads of southern Alabama en route to Fort Rucker, the home of US Army aviation. I can't recall which course I was attending there, but it was something that necessitated pulling me out of my unit to get some additional higher education. I had the Camaro's top down and was just rowing through the gears when I saw them. A set of wires had somehow escaped my scan and I was about to hit them. I slammed on the brakes and veered to avoid flying into them. As the car's nose came around in a hair-raising slide down the road, I realised – too late for me and my buddy's Z-car – that I was not flying, but driving! The wires were *supposed* to be up there. I guess that when you get that 'edge', it tends to be there always, even when you are supposed to be enjoying a nice country drive.

Those young warrant officer pilots were scouts – whose mission is particularly hairy. While I was cranking my ill-fated 139 that morning, I saw and heard their helicopters arriving. Behind my aircraft were several concrete revetments where their small OH-58D 'Deltas' (simply called 'Deltas' in local army speak) were parked. They had come hovering up the taxiway in a dusty cloud of rotor wash and passed behind me to my left before hovering carefully into their concrete enclosures, which were designed to take indirect fire and minimise blast damage. Following their cool down and shutdown, they had collected their things and were done for the day.

The scouts' mission is to seek out the enemy. So how do they do that, exactly? Well, that's where the 'hairy' part comes into play. They fly low around areas of suspected enemy activity and try to entice those on the ground to shoot at them. That's right – they seek and draw fire. They travel together and array themselves in such a manner as to be mutually supporting. If one is engaged by the enemy, the number two aircraft is seconds away from placing deadly fire onto the shooter. If everything works out well, the engaged crew escapes the initial volley using rapid manoeuvres, putting their training into practice, while their wingman weighs in on the shooter/s and assists him/them to exit this life. Unfortunately, for a brave few, (too many more than a few), those first rounds occasionally find their mark. The results from such scenarios are somewhat different, although from what I have seen and heard, the end result for the enemy is generally always the same. When we have a downed bird, the fight sometimes grows into a pretty big deal.

One thing I have noticed when talking to these guys – these aeroscouts – is that they look directly into your eyes when talking, although they won't talk about the flying unless they are comfortable with you as a fellow pilot. They don't smile as much as other pilots over in this theatre. They live a hard life both on and off the battlefield. Their commander told me proudly that his pilots had accounted for many kills over here and were fearless in battle. I'd have to agree.

I know a little about pushing a fight. I have done it a few times myself. When you really need to know if the guys in that truck over there are going to shoot at you or not, you might as well do it on your terms and not theirs. After all, you're there to fight, so why waste perfectly good daylight?

When I was flying the Huey gunship, we would 'bump' on potential targets. When a gunner called out a potential target or we spied something suspicious, we carried out a manoeuvre we called a bump to give our guys a good shot. This involves flying straight at the target, then pulling slightly away from it to the side, although the position of your wingman and the terrain might some-times call for an opposite turn. A little offset allows the gunner an early shot if action starts before you are in the manoeuvre. When you are in the right spot, you pull aft stick, pitch the nose up and bleed airspeed. As the speed comes back and you reach the optimal range to the target, you start rolling towards it. This forces you to fly the aircraft while literally looking over your shoulder.

If flown correctly, the manoeuvre looks like you are flying an arch over a point in the ground. Then, with fine adjustments to the pedals, you can literally 'walk' the fire onto the target. Although it means the aircraft is slowing all the time, making it increasingly vulnerable, it gives the gunner an easy shot. Essen-tially, you are betting your life on the ability of the guy on the trigger behind you to get 'him' before he gets you.

With a section of two aircraft, the moment number two calls "In", you turn out and away in a diving turning manoeuvre to set up to cover his pull off. Hell, if he missed also, something was going wrong, but that's how it's done. On some nights when I was number two, when bumping into the fight, all I could see in front of me was a shower of bullets, with their tracer elements bouncing up in front of the aircraft's nose. It is a beautiful sight – until you realise what all those little things are. However, in all the times I have done it, the only damage my aircraft ever received was from our own brass flying back and striking the tail rotor blades. But that is another story, for another time.

Anyway, the people down in the Helmand valley know what it means for the helicopter to pop up over them. The next sound is likely to be the mini gun – followed by the fat lady singing 'game over'. So if you pull a bump over anything suspicious, they are thinking: OK, two seconds to paradise. Which makes it into a 'use it or lose it' deal for them and, if they are enemy, they sometimes feel obliged to open fire. Most times, however, we'd just cut some fun holes in the sky and nothing would happen.

Today's aeroscouts also employ the bump, although they do it head on, as they have direct-fire, cockpit-aimed weapons. They are a different breed, indeed. If they were infantry, they would be rangers. If they were shooters, they would be snipers. What they are, in their company of aerial warriors, is a mixture of Southern-fried patriotism and steely-eyed killers. With the eyes of eagles and the hearts of saints, they shoulder the safety of a nation; they are, simply, the best.

Chapter 21

O' DARK-THIRTY

Man, I hate these early mornings! I haven't been to a single briefing in the light of the day and every day is just another in an endless procession of similar activities. This rotation has been hellish in more ways than one. It isn't even six in the morning and already, I'm staggering into the brightly-lit briefing room, which is such a stark contrast to the darkness outside. With the coldness of its unshielded fluorescent tubes above, and its matching unpainted plywood walls and floor, it is not a comfortable place. The day started more than an hour ago when the electronic beeping of the cheap plastic army alarm clock pulled me out of a deep sleep.

The seats in the briefing room are the cheapo plastic folding kind with tubular metal frames. There are two rows, each with six seats, in the small plywood room, which has a forty-seven-inch flat screen TV centred in the front. Every morning, I try to grab the seat closest to the wall so I can lean against the dusty plywood and get a bit more comfortable. On most mornings, my eyes are irritated and teary from the combination of lack of sleep and the dust that is always hanging in the air. Somewhere around 0600, the briefing begins. As I look over the weather report, I wonder just how wrong it is going to be today. The visibility block is listing quad nines, which means unlimited visibility. However, I remember being unable to see Three-Mile Mountain, which is less than three miles from us, so the visibility is clearly not right. I wonder what other relevant facts are also incorrect.

The briefing officer starts going over the mission details and talking about the other traffic that will be flying along our route (as if I will ever see them). Many people think of airspace only in two-dimensional terms, so that if two lines cross, it must automatically mean a 'mid-air'. However, we aviators fly all over the place, usually nowhere near our planned route. So firstly, we are probably not going to be exactly where we said we were going to be, and secondly, one of us will be down low at 500 feet above ground level, and the other will be half a mile above it. Most of the time, you never see the other guy.

It was much worse when I flew jets. If ATC reported my traffic as some low-level helicopter along the river at 1,000 feet, I didn't have a snowball's chance in hell of ever seeing him out of my smallish windows, with my airspeed dial reading 250 or better. He might be looking right at me, but for me, he was just a quickly disappearing blue or yellow dot on my TCAS (traffic collision avoidance system) screen. As it happens, I have a TCAS in my current helicopter, which is nice, so that when ATC reports traffic to me, I reply: "Roger that; I have him on the fish finder."

After the traffic flow part of the briefing comes the threat brief. This is where I really start to pay attention. If I have a napkin handy, this is when I use it to blot out the tears so I can focus better on all the red squares and circles. The geometric shapes give clues as to the nature of threats, but anything coloured red, just like in civilian life, is not good. Today, as with most days, the relationship between the red, the yellow and the clear areas was just about right. During the briefing, the officer talked about a marine KIA (killed in action) over in the Helmand valley and some other things, but made no mention of anything else going on. There were a couple of oddities and eyebrow raisers here and there, but mostly, it looked like a go for another day of flying.

With the threat brief out of the way, it was finally off to the mess hall for some mystery meat and vulcanized eggs with some turpentine coffee to wash it all down.

The run-up and take-off was normal, except that Chalk Two unexpectedly needed fuel before departure. That added another fifteen minutes to our timeline, which would also push everything else back for the rest of the day. There must have been some extensive maintenance requiring ground runs the day before, or that helicopter would have had a nearly full tank. Never mind. I remembered some advice given to me by an experienced aviator a couple of decades earlier about the three most useless things to a pilot: runway behind you, altitude above you, and fuel left in the truck. I submitted to the wisdom of the past and decided to get some gas too.

Our first destination was a nearby FOB (forward operating base) only about ten minutes away. Virtually as soon as we cleared the Kandahar airspace, I had to change to the tactical frequency for the nearby FOB to request entry. Immediately upon switching frequencies, we were inundated with busy chatter. We lis-

Above: The Red Desert just south west of Kandahar. This area was relatively peaceful although on the other side of the hill on the left, it was 'Game-on'.

Left: UH-1 Huey 2 showing camouflage paint scheme and gunner with a M240 machine gun at altitude. These aircraft were former US Army 'H' model Hueys which served in Vietnam. They were highly modified with a much more powerful 1,800-horsepower engine, a different main rotor and tail rotor, a larger tail boom and other differences. They remain very capable and rugged helicopters.

Left: Our U-1H Super Hueys sitting in the 'Old Hangar' adjacent to 'kilo ramp' on KAF. You can see where the bombs came through and blew away much of the roof, siding and all of the windows.

Below: UH-1H (II) Super Huey in flight south of Ghazni.

Top left: Jason Hallmark with his favorite 'toy' and a mechanic running pre-flight checks of his weapon. Jason and his brother 'Geeb' were amongst the best gunners that the program had produced. An ex-marine he was the lead gunner and a great guy to have around.

Top right: Author with typical flight and protective gear. Wearing both an M9, 9mm pistol and carrying a Colt M4 carbine. Vest includes a medical kit, tourniquet, extra bandages, a radio, 6x30 round M4 magazines 3x9-mm pistol magazines, a GPS, signaling devices, Kevlar and armour plates, compass, extra batteries, a space blanket, fire starter, flashlight, and a couple of packs of chewing gum! Also shown is the same silk scarf the author wore on almost every flight for many years, which he wou bring home to launder then have his wife wear it before taking it back to the war.

Above left: 155-mm gun; capable of firing a very heavy projectile extremely long distances to pi point accuracy. They are the heavy-duty artillery workhorse. Next step up from this is somethi released from a wing store at altitude. *(US Defense Department)*

Above right: Super Huey2 in flight up around 10,000 feet overflying a foggy valley in easte Afghanistan.

Bottom right: John 'New Guy' Sable. He was the air mission commander for what turned out be a few gunfights with the Taliban. A Louisiana-born 'southern boy', John was also a former pol officer, and had served almost twenty years as a US Army aeroscout pilot.

Top left: A pair of Dutch AH-64 attack helicopters loaded down with ordnance. These two had to fly out and destroy some US vehicles which were badly damaged in an ambush near Tarin Kowt (TK).

Middle left: Super Huey on the take-off roll. Rotor blades are heavily coned from the maximum gross weight that the aircraft is often called upon to carry. Kandahar, 2007.

Lower middle left: Bullet hole in the tail boom. This aircraft miraculously stayed aloft even though the tail rotor control push-pull rod had been nearly shot in two.

Bottom left: Bullet hole in the main rotor control tube. A failure of this tube would have caused total loss of main rotor control and a violent crash.

Bottom right: Author holding a roll of '100-mph' tape which was severed by an AK-47 bullet. The gunner who was onboard and had so many bullets strike all around him is looking on.

Top left: This aircraft took so many hits that it was deemed 'combat ineffective' and was no longer useable. The aircraft was, however, repaired the following day and flown back to Kandahar where it underwent a complete replacement of all the battle-damaged parts it had sustained.

Top right: SAR medics Pete Vanderspuy and Jon Pearman who, amazingly, flew over 250 hours a month during the poppy seed harvest in 2007. Pete was former South African Special Forces and Jon a former US 'Green Beret'. They were both highly-qualified medics, but also deadly in a gunfight.

Above left: SAR bird hot refuelling at Ghazni, Afghanistan. Pete is holding the hose, helping the US Army refueller, while Jon actually pumps the gas. Our guys liked to do things like this themselves. They always watched over all of us and the aircraft.

Above right: SAR bird perched on nearby pinnacle of dirt and rock with Dick Edington at the controls.

Left: Author standing outside the cockpit taking a breather during an escort mission. Outside temperature was around forty-five degrees Celsius!

Rifle. This weapon could, as some would say, "reach out and touch someone".

Above right: One of the SAR medics with his 'Game Face' on. All the SAR medics were ex-special forces, seals, rangers and all had numerous combat tours of duty under their belt before showing up for this program.

Above left: GAU-17 electric mini gun. This weapon is a game changer. It puts out 3,000 rounds per minute from six barrels. When flying, sometimes, the gunners would fire forward putting the muzzle a couple of feet from the pilot. Being there with that gun ripping the very fabric of space apart that close was truly an out of body experience.

Top: John 'New Guy' Sable at the controls while sitting on the ground at idle. SAR medics have taken up positions around the bird maintaining a watchful eye on the terrain around us.

Middle left: SAR medics. Weapon in foreground is a modernised US M14 7.62x51

Above left: While perched in an overwatch position close to the border of Uzbekistan with my gunship at idle, Geeb, brother to Jason Hallmark, walks the perimeter just to make sure no one is sneaking up on us.

Above right: Gunship perched in an overwatch position during an active raid type of mission which is taking place thousands of feet below in a village in the valley. During this mission the heavy gun bird with its mini guns is cruising over the target area ready to provide instant gunship support. The author's aircraft was configured as a 'light gun', with less armament, so it can be used also in an emergency swoop; to land and carry out wounded or even captured enemy forces.

Left: Worn out pilot walking through the rotor blast of another aircraft. Both are returning after a long day of escort duty.

Top: Huey SAR bird overlooking a town where an operation against enemy forces is ongoing. Should someone be wounded, that bird would spin up and fly immediately to the scene. Sitting on the ground at idle saves gas that might be needed to transport a casualty to a hospital.

Above left: MJ and I relaxing after a long hot day of flying. MJ was a 'Cool Hand'. A southern Alabama 'boy' who loves boating and talked in a slow, measured manner, exuding his southern accent. He could always be counted on to execute his mission with precision and safety. I relied on him often.

Above right: Mi–8 accident at KAF, 2010. Aircraft started up in gusty wind conditions. The blade flexed down into the tail boom. A crewmember standing outside was fatally wounded during the event. Our aircraft routinely operated with former Russian military crews on this exact ramp.

Left: Sunset in Kandahar.

Top: British Lynx helicopters parked on the 'Brit Ramp' adjacent to ours. These aircraft flew many sorties in the cooler months but somewhat less when it was hot.

in the spring time. The poppy is the light, almost white appearance in the fields.

Above right: Suspicious activity near this ditch in the road led us to take a closer look. An IED was found near the water pump and later blown up by engineers. View is from 500 feet while circling the area when the bomb was first discovered.

Left: Gereshk FOB in the Helmand valley, a highly contested area. Fighting takes place almost daily near this camp. For us it was an oasis of rest and a warm lunch on the days that would allow it. It is also called FOB Price, named after US Army Special Forces Chief Warrant Officer Price who died while stationed there. Several of the author's letters are written about this place.

Top: Typical possible Taliban sighting. Sometimes they would fight and other times, as in this instance, they simply move into the fields in the background to harvest or tend to the poppy crop.

Above left: Poppy fields in bloom. Although this plant later will produce ninety-seven percent of the world's heroin, the plant itself and the thousands of fields growing it are spectacular in their beauty

Above: Poppy eradication forces in the fields. The quads dug around pipes which fractured the plants. I observed this activity over the years and would have to say, that despite our honest efforts we were mostly ineffective in stopping heroin production at this level. Sometimes I'd see one of our tractors dig under the plant, then watch villagers quickly replanting the 'destroyed' plant within minutes. Later in a couple months I'd actually see villagers and Taliban actually harvesting the same plant!

Middle: Friendly convoy moving across the desert near the Helmand valley.

Bottom ANPs or Afghan National Police. They did what they could to stabilise the area, but their ranks were thoroughly infiltrated by Taliban sympathisers at that time, rendering them far less effective, and creating a very dangerous environment for those of us who supported them.

Above: Entrance of one of the three passes through the southern wall of the Hindu Kush mountains just north west of Bagram Air Force Base. This valley floor rises to just over 10,000 feet, whereas the other passes lie at around 11,000 feet and 12,400 feet respectively.

Middle: Southern edge of Hindu Kush mountains just north of Bagram Air Force Base.

Bottom: M240 gunner manning his weapon in flight. The trick is to cover every part of your body in an, often failed, attempt to stay warm. Sometimes we flew missions at temperatures well below zero degrees. Unfortunately, the doors had to stay open to allow for effective engagements with the various weapon systems.

Top: UH-1 Super Huey high up in the Hindu Kush mountain range. These mountains are the foot hills of the Himalayas and rise to around 17,000 feet in this area.

Above left: Early spring plantings come to life north of Kunduz about forty miles south of Uzbekistan. We have just launched for a raid on a target about fifty miles away.

Above right: Flying low, gunners keeping a close watch over the Kandahar desert.

Left: The author at the controls of a Super Huey with his wife's scarf sticking out of the flight suit. It was used to keep the skin on his neck from rubbing raw when constantly turning his head looking for signs of the enemy.

Top and middle left: Gunners jammed into aft seats of their Bell 412s always scanning their sectors while flying low and fast. This was taken in early 2009 on a mission flown out of Kirkuk, Iraq. The gunner is a young man recently out of the army who had served a tour in Iraq as a soldier. He was then trained privately as a door gunner. These guys scanned their sectors while we flew at around 35-50 feet at 130 knots. Their job was to suppress enemy forces with their weapons to keep them from hitting us.

Middle right: Bell 412 helicopter flying very low in northern Iraq.

Above right: Typical gunner's station in one of the many civilian aircraft which have been 'militarized' by the contract companies employing them. This aircraft, a Bell Helicopters product, is set up for use with an M4 carbine.

Top: Red Cross US Army Medevac UH-60 Blackhawk on the ready pad at Kandahar Air Field circa 2006. In the background is three-mile mountain, an ominous ridge separating the airbase from the city of Kandahar.

Above: Chinook helicopters, produced by Boeing, have huge power reserves and can carry substantial loads. A magnificent helicopter, these Dutch Chinooks are accompanied by two of their 'Cougar' helicopters, a modernised version of the venerable Puma.

Middle left: Typical arrangement inside a Chinook, with a gunner on the right door, an observer on the left window and a passenger or possibly a third pilot in the jump seat in the narrow walkway into the cockpit.

Bottom left: Apache aircraft from the Arizona national guard; you can see the very obvious state flag on the vertical fin above the tail rotor. Although 'part time warriors' they proved to be pit bulls on the battlefield.

Top and Above: British C130 that hit a land mine actually embedded in the runway at Lashkar Gah, Afghanistan. The exploding mine caused the aircraft to catch fire and burn to the ground. The crew and passengers, which included the British Ambassador to Afghanistan and a number of SBS troops were evacuated but the C130 was destroyed. A couple of months earlier a Russian AN-32 crashed there also killing the whole crew and several villagers as it skidded off the runway.

Above left: Typical 'urban sprawl'. Possibly southern part of Kabul, their 'modern' city.

Above right: Typical Afghan farmer.

Middle left: Typical Afghan family.

Below left: A Bedouin camp. As nomads they may migrate into the Red Desert during the winter, then back into the wadi areas when the temperatures began to climb around April.

Main picture: Author with the hot wind blowing in Afghanistan, 2006.

Inset left: The author always kept this picture of his wife, Kathy, and their boys on his wall.

Inset right: The author's three girls: Allison, Heather, and Jessica, Easter 2010.

tened as two Kiowa Warrior helicopters called inbound for fuel and rearming. Hmmm, that didn't sound normal. I called in, reported our position and requested permission to enter the ROZ. The lead Kiowa Warrior pilot asked me to stay clear for a moment while he and his wingman made their approach. He said they were in a TIC (troops in contact), which basically meant he was in the middle of a gunfight. I complied and asked where the fight was. He told me it was just north of the FOB. That certainly hadn't been discussed during our earlier briefing.

Finally, we were cleared in and landed. We dropped off our troops and departed for the next of three destinations on the first run of the day. Again, we talked to several folks on the tactical push (frequency) and got permission to land at our second location. This particular outpost was manned by a joint NATO force with only a few Americans present. We lined the approach up on a patch of dirt, which seemed more or less undisturbed outside the wire. The 'wire', as we refer to it, can be literally strands of razor or concertina barbed wire, or it can be a wall or a row of huge dirt-filled Hesco barriers forming a continuous wall.

The thought occurred to me that this patch of dirt might have been a mine field, until I realised that numerous piles of gravel nearby meant that the corps of engineers were very soon going to turn this spot into a HLZ (helicopter landing zone). I liked the spot for a couple of reasons; not only because I thought it would produce less dust, but also because it was situated right on a bluff with a drop of about 100 feet along its back side. This meant no one could sneak up on us from behind and the gunners in the watchtower had clear views of everything else.

We waited some time before a sergeant and a corporal made their way outside. They were moving in a crouched position with their weapons at the ready. That was strange; I was supposed to pick up five soldiers, but only two were approaching – and doing so in a tactical manner. The staff sergeant told me there was no one to pick up here and, more interestingly, that there were enemy around. He pointed to a spot near the drop behind the helicopter and explained that they had been probed last night from that exact spot. He told me to get out of the area because it wasn't safe at the moment. I couldn't help wondering why the intelligence officer had missed that vital piece of information as well.

So far, we had flown to two destinations, and both were hot areas with enemy activity in the vicinity. As we pulled pitch and headed north for the final destination of our first leg of the day, I felt I should have been given a heads up about these two situations.

When we arrived at location three, I landed at one location to drop off cargo, while the other helicopter went into the primary LZ where he was supposed to pick up eight troops. After dropping off my cargo, I began heading to the primary LZ to join our number two and pick up any remaining personnel. As I approached low from the north, Two called off and clear. When I asked him if we needed to stop and pick up anyone else, he replied that he had one person and that was all that would be coming. As we climbed to altitude, I asked why there was only one guy. They replied the soldier's squad had been hit with an improvised explosive device, and had suffered a KIA and had many wounded; this one soldier was the only one left.

A KIA – and the briefer didn't know about that either? I started to get a crawling feeling way down low in the spine – a sense of impending danger; I had seen enough. We were briefed for a day that should have been a 'walk in the park', but every destination we had gone to so far had been seriously infected with a bad case of enemy. The next planned destination had actually been briefed as being hostile. The intelligence officer had made the comment that she didn't actually think anything was going to happen there but, from what I was seeing, I wasn't getting that vibe. We decided to call the rest of the flight off until I could get some better information and figure out why our briefing had been so wrong.

When we got back to base, it was still quite early in the morning – although early is a relative term. I'm not talking 0600, but it was still well before I prefer to get up if given the choice. When I go home and play domestic Don, there is no getting up early, or at any specific time for that matter. There is no way I'll have anything to do with schedules, busy days or meetings. I like to wake up late, start off slowly, and then let the rest of the day gradually taper off from there. But now, here we were headed back to base and it was just past nine – still technically eligible to be considered time for a late breakfast coffee. (Which sounded like a much safer plan than firing up those helos again and going back out for another turn or two.)

But that was not going to happen. Every time I think about not flying, I immediately think of all those kids – those young soldiers – out there on the line. We carry all sorts of things for them, from implements of war to milk and mail. Just about every imaginable commodity has graced the inside of our aircraft one time or another. That's one of the great things about flying a 'utility' mission. You never know what's coming next. I remember the line in Forrest Gump: "Life is like a box of chocolates; you never know what you're going to get next." I love that line, and it describes our mission perfectly.

Now, on some of those sorties, it is possible to make the big score. For example, when we're carrying boxes of fresh grapes along with machine-gun parts, it isn't unheard of for one of those boxes of grapes to be somehow 'misplaced'. Back in my army days, when I flew the Chinook, this practice was commonly known as 'air tax'. Fly the venerable Chinook and you're never out of milk, cookies, fruit, candy, cake and every other fattening thing known to modern man! Good old air tax – a concept that happily lives on in the back roads and battle corridors of Afghanistan to this very day.

The taxed do not seem to mind it all that much. After all, they see us as crazy people. They think we are mentally deficient for flying around in thin-skinned moving targets while they sit in revetments. However, conversely, we – the flying few – think they are the crazy ones. I only have to see one tracer come zipping by my cockpit window to realise I don't have to stay – I can fly away from this nasty place, but those grunts down there get to live in it 24/7.

Back to the mission. After taking a fresh look at the situation, and informing a very surprised intelligence officer, we launched for the rest of the day's missions. We bypassed the one questionable destination but we managed to get around to everything else. I would be rotating home in just a couple days, so the thought of getting shot with only a couple days left in country was bouncing around in my mind as we banked and flew through the mountains and down long, winding valleys.

The best time to get shot, if there is such a thing, is considered to be when you have just arrived in the country. That way, you don't have to suffer through all the junk that is certain to come your way: sickness, sleepless nights, loneliness, lousy food, the smell and...well, I assume you get the picture. No. Show up, do a day or two, take a flesh wound and get sent home to a hero's welcome. That's much better than hanging out until the day before you're due to leave, then getting sent to some evacuation hospital in Germany.

After about seven hours, we were taxiing the dusty birds back on the aluminium matting installed directly over dirt that made up the runway and taxiways of our tactical airfield. Clicking along, it felt good to be done. The day's count would be sixty-odd troops and more than 10,000 lbs of cargo pushed out to LZs all over southern Afghanistan. The birds had served us well and had returned in a reusable condition. The latter is very important to mechanics, but not so much for pilots. To us, we use what we need and put the things to bed. The poor mechanics then pore over them with soft cotton cloths, wiping away the dirt and grease, and taking care to adjust this and tighten that. They do this in a Groundhog Day-type ritual that never ends and usually goes well into the night. That is their night, but it is not mine.

My night is reserved for crawling into that glorious bunk for some well-earned shuteye. No matter that the mattress is flat and is cheaply made. If you are sleeping, you are not really here or there. You get to be somewhere else very far away. You get to dance across the waves or dance with your favourite lady. Dreamland is probably the only place I can think of that is possibly wilder than where my day-to-day job is, but it is also as settling as a fresh snowfall. So as the sleep overtakes you, the dust drifts slowly away and the soreness abates, there is no more fear of a fiery crash or constantly having to scan for movement in the shadows below you. The hissing of static on the intercom is gradually replaced by a whisper in your ear in that sleepy dream state. The battle cry is gone and all there is left is a gentle breeze peacefully raking through the Kentucky blue-grass of my home, so very far away.

Chapter 22

WISDOM

I consider myself to have been very fortunate. For a start, I believe that to have been selected to become an army aviator was probably more than I deserved. Then, having served an entire career, to have retired, become a civilian and subsequently continued to fly for several more years (far longer than I ever imagined, way back when) – especially when it's something I'm still doing – has all been one big blessing.

One can't do all that I have been fortunate to do, or experience all that I have experienced, without learning a few things along the way.

I was sitting at my big family-built walnut desk at home, recently, thinking about the past, my good fortune and what an amazing experience life has been, and figured it would be a good idea to write down some of the things I have learned along the way. I guess when you are closer to the far end of life than the beginning, you often think of such things, at least I have been, lately. Throughout my life, I have learned many things I perceive to be truths, which, dare I suggest it, one could consider to be called 'wisdom'. Perhaps. Certainly, as far as I am concerned, they all ring with truth. Here are a few pearls of my personal wisdom; take from them what you will. Enjoy.

When tackling a tough task, always surround yourself with people who are smarter than you, which is easy because most are.

The fuel gauge is not always correct.

Don't tempt fate.

Never recon anything you can send infantry to recon first. Never send infantry to recon anything you can shoot with artillery first.

No matter what you do, someone, somewhere is probably filming it.

You are not smarter than the enemy.

Plan for every conceivable contingency – then depart with the conviction that something you know nothing about will occur when you least expect it.

When the enemy is in range, so are you!

Don't wait until tomorrow to say you're sorry.

Never, ever tell a lie; it will come back to haunt you as long as you live.

Don't save a good bottle, a good joke or an apology for tomorrow.

Live for today – it could be all you have.

Live life hard, get your hands dirty, play often and love as much as you can.

Do favours and good deeds in secret.

If you get that sneaking suspicion, or that funny little feeling about something, pay attention.

There is no such thing as an impossible shot, especially if your adversary is doing the shooting.

God really is your co-pilot.

If you think being a pilot makes you better than others, you're wrong, and they all know it.

It is possible for an entire burst of automatic fire to miss you by less than six inches.

Before going off to war, make plans to return. Then, when you get there, forget all about them.

You **can** fly straight through a pine tree.

A tank cannon pointed right at you is at least ten feet in diameter.

In combat, aircraft systems' instruments are just extra weight. In fact, so is anything else that doesn't contribute to speed.

Never purposely do anything to make yourself famous.

During your youth, make sure to create a few 'rocking chair' stories – but just a few!

Tracer rounds float lazily up toward you then pass by at almost the speed of light.

Light on the battlefield is usually not good – it attracts other, more dangerous, kinds of light.

If you are the highest-ranking individual and everyone is counting on you, you are in serious trouble.

Make a decision and stick with it. It is usually wrong, so changing it makes you look even worse.

When doing a night dust landing in a helicopter, no one will be where they were supposed to be, including you.

When combat flying at low level, the enemy will shoot at you with small arms. Get a little higher and they use bigger stuff. Go even higher and they shoot missiles. I say, just do whatever you want and try to have a good time doing it.

I heard this one often and it's true: no plan remains intact following contact.

An entire grass hut can pass right through the rotor system of a Chinook.

A single 90-mm anti-tank round will cause a grass hut to take off vertically.

Rotor blades don't do well with grass huts and pine trees!

Don't wait until night to say your prayers.

Sometimes an aircraft will keep going if you just talk to it.

It sucks having grey hair; people somehow think you know what you're doing.

It's great having grey hair; people somehow think you know what you're doing.

A positive attitude really does fix things.

The good news is that the AK-47 is probably the best assault rifle in the world. The bad news is that we don't have it – they do.

If you tear up when you see your flag hoisted, you are a patriot. If you shed a tear when you see a flag-draped coffin, you've been blessed.

If you volunteer, you will get picked.

Don't ask, 'Why him and not me?' It is a question with no answer.

If you're on fire and there is a ship there, land on it.

If you go looking for trouble, the odds are you'll find it.

Night vision goggles do not work unless you turn them on.

If you want a life of plenty, then learn to give.

If you 'simulate' an engine failure during training, I promise you that, eventually it will not be simulated.

Making a gear-up belly landing on a lovely smooth grassy field in a B-17 is not that hard, according to my Dad. However, he assures me it becomes more complicated when there is a six-foot-deep ditch in the field.

If someone offers you a hand, take it.

Look people directly in the eyes when telling them tough things, even when it's the sister of a fellow soldier and you have to tell her that he fell and you didn't.

Don't spend too much time trying to figure out why.

Have two or three good friends – and keep them.

Smile a lot.

You have two ears and one mouth – consider the ratio!

If you're married, you're lucky. If you have children, you're blessed.

Chapter 23

NEVER
VOLUNTEER

Through my previous letters you will already be familiar with my good friend Matt. This particular Matt story took place in the mid-nineties and began back at sunny Fort Campbell, Kentucky, where we were stationed together. Matt was the company's safety officer and I was its standardisation instructor pilot, a sort of a catch-all flight standards/operations/lead pilot guy.

Our hero Matt had just been promoted to the rank of chief warrant officer 4 (CW4) in the US Army. CW4 is a lofty rank indeed within the brotherhood of the warrant officer corps, which extends from CW1 to CW5. As a CW4, Matt was nearing the top, and was considered to be a highly-experienced aviator of considerable knowledge and wisdom. Warrant officers are a breed apart from their commissioned officer counterparts. Commissioned officers – the lieutenants, captains, majors, colonels and so forth – are raised as leaders, commanders and decision makers, while warrant officers are technical specialists and do not necessarily command or lead troops in battle.

However, this concept is turned on its head in US Army aviation, where warrant officers are the actual aircraft commanders, flight leads, trainers and air mission commanders, and, in many instances, serve in a variety of other crucial command and staff positions. The warrant officers are the guys who plan missions, fly the aircraft, get people where they need to be on time, and decide who to blast and who to medevac. By the time one becomes a CW4, one is entrusted to make big decisions and make them competently.

Army aviation placed its warrant officer pilots into three broad categories at that time: 'Standards' included all the instructor pilots and operations guys and 'Maintenance' was where you found the test pilots, while 'Safety' (Matt's position at the time of this story) was where the single company, battalion or brigade safety officer lived.

Nearing the end of my military career, I was the 'silverback' in the company and my CW4 bar was looking worn and dated, having graced my hat for six years. I was not only the senior warrant officer in the company, but was also the senior warrant officer for the entire battalion of 48 CH-47D Chinook helicopters. Matt was just starting his journey as a 'silverback' and was looking for a chance to make his mark – something he would soon do in a most unusual way, doing something completely unexpected.

It all started during the initial briefing for an upcoming JRTC (joint readiness training command) exercise that is conducted at Fort Polk, Louisiana – home to most of the nastiest venomous insects and snakes on earth. I am sure that, just like in the Amazon, there are many species of man-killers there which have not yet been classified but which routinely dine on soldiers of the US Army.

All of the officers, around thirty-eight of them or so, sat in the 'lizard lounge' (a large briefing area outside flight operations and Matt's and my offices) while the major in command gave us the general overview. While the major went on about dates, goals, desires and facts about this and that, Matt and I quietly discussed who would actually do what in the upcoming field exercise.

Matt was sometimes given to acting impulsively, as might be remembered from previous letters, and this tendency was about to bite him directly in the hindquarters. During his presentation, the major announced that he wanted a volunteer to be the infantry liaison officer – a request that sat as flat as a two-day-old pancake. No one who was sitting there moved a muscle, lest any such movement might be noticed and mistaken for volunteering. The major's gaze passed from one side of the room to the other in a scan much like that of a southern Baptist preacher during an altar call. Eventually, his eyes locked upon me. I knew the major well from many closed-door discussions and his look was unmistakable: "Help me, please; I'm getting killed up here." I was about to stand and say something about being a man and stepping up to the plate – words I would have struggled with, because I definitely did not believe them whole-heartedly – when Matt blurted out: "Sir, I'll do it!"

Everyone turned to stare at my little friend sitting beside me. The major's face had changed to a "What in bloody hell?" sort of look and there was widespread confusion amongst the younger pilots. You see, a CW4 does not need to volunteer for anything. He is the old guy; he outranks practically everyone and has already paid his dues during a decade or two of service. But Matt wasn't kidding. He stood up and said, "Sir, I'll show some leadership. I'll do it; I'll be the infantry liaison!"

The major was clearly dumfounded; after looking briefly at Matt in stunned surprise, his eyes fell on me once more. This time, the look he gave me asked the question, "Are you screwing with me?" I distanced myself slightly from Matt – in order to be clear of the proverbial blast area – and gave my commander a shoulder shrug. The major just nodded and said simply, "All right, Matt, you've got it."

As I looked at the faces of the young officers all around me, I noted they looked relieved and confused. They realised they had dodged a big one and that they would get to fly. As such, they would be subject to the crew rest policies that guaranteed them dry, comfortable places to live and sleep. They knew that the poor sucker who went out with the infantry would not fly at all. Furthermore, they knew he would live with the grunts doing all that they did – which was moving all the time, never sleeping, never washing, seldom eating and having no more comfort than that which they could garner from a rucksack crammed full of ammunition and essential equipment.

Matt was screwed; he had just 'shot himself in the foot' – maybe even both feet. What was it he had just displayed? Was it courage, or foolishness? Anyway, the major had little else to say to the group and dismissed them. As he did so, he gave me a wave, which signalled that he wanted to talk to me in private. After the major had left the room and the operations officer had stood us at ease, I turned to face Matt. Returning my incredulous stare, in full-on Matt style, he demanded simply, "What?" I could only chuckle at the man as he stood there. He may have been slightly built and short, but he had a heart as big as Texas and courage to match. Acting on heart-felt emotion, he had just committed himself to several weeks of utter misery, although I suspect the enormity of his actions hadn't sunk in yet. "Don, did I just screw up?" he asked me. "Yep, more than you will ever know," I think I replied. However, it didn't matter; the damage was done and events were already in motion that would directly affect my younger friend.

Of course, the major wanted to talk to me about the 'Matt deal' as it became known. "Is that guy serious? Does he realise he doesn't have to do this? I can recall him on the grounds that he is the safety officer and get him out of it." I suggested to the major that in life, we all have to learn some valuable lessons first-hand, and Matt would learn this lesson best if he went through with it. "Well, all right. But I'll be dammed – I never suspected that one for a second!"

As the days at Fort Campbell waned and the day for deployment drew closer, Matt no longer wore a green pickle suit but donned the infantry's BDU (battle dress uniform). He traded in his Chinook helicopter for a trusty Humvee festooned with radios and, during the dark nights preceding the deployment, he practised his new craft of planning missions, and directing PZs (pick-up zones) – the locations where helicopters collect the various loads they have to carry to the battlefield.

The 101st Airborne to which we were assigned was the army's only air assault division. It was, by far, the most expensive division in the entire US Army, fielding an impressive 450 helicopters. It was a super-aggressive unit designed to project great combat power more than 100 miles into enemy territory. With our Chinooks, we could pick up loads of up to 18,000 lb and fly them – at low level, in very low light, with pinpoint accuracy – to arrive within thirty seconds of an assigned time. Of course, much of this hinged on how smoothly the PZ was operating, a gargantuan task that now depended directly on Matt.

Finally, the day came and we all launched from Fort Campbell and flew south toward central Louisiana, a flight of 700 miles, which I had planned to incorporate three segments. During the first leg, everyone flew at 500 feet in several large formations down to Memphis, Tennessee. This allowed the guys to hone their formation flying skills during daylight. From Memphis to a point in northern Louisiana, we each filed IFR and climbed into the clouds like airline pilot wannabes. No one knew it, but I had arranged for a big barbecue for everyone at our next stop; as we landed, we enjoyed freshly cooked hotdogs, hamburgers and chicken. The final leg into our 'objective' – an airbase near Fort Polk Army Airfield – was flown at night using night vision goggles. Matt actually manned the controls as a reward for all his hard work during the three legs down to Polk. It was to be his last time at the controls for a long time, though, and upon arrival at the JRTC, he disappeared to join his infantry brigade.

We were all soon busy with planning, briefings and fitting laser sensors to our aircraft. (At JRTC, the 'weapons' were fitted with lasers; this necessitated fitting one's uniform, vehicle and aircraft with sensors to record any hits.)

It wasn't long – a couple of days, perhaps – before we were ordered to deploy to our field location; a large open sandy area in the north-east corner of the manoeuvre box. Upon landing, we began setting up tents and our personal areas, as well as digging foxholes and placing barbed wire everywhere. As we continued to assume a 'battle posture', reports of 'insurgent' activity began to come in. The 101st was given the mission of assisting the national forces of 'Tasmania' (or something like that) to remove and destroy a growing insurgent army to allow peace and democracy to return. OK. It was game on – this is what we all lived for. If we couldn't kill bad guys for real, then at least we could practise doing it.

I was the flight lead for the initial air assault mission – an impressive show of force involving seventy-five helicopters and several thousand troops. As I arrived at the PZ, I heard Matt's voice directing the various aircraft about and coordinating the business of moving loads. We didn't know it until later, but one of the Humvees we lifted was actually Matt's and he rode in the darkened cabin of our aircraft amongst his new-found infantry friends. He was already much thinner than he had been and his blackened face was almost covered by the Kevlar helmet that was now a regular part of his dress. He had definitely changed. While he was no longer a pilot, he was still not yet infantry either; he was somewhere between those two worlds.

As the operation progressed and developed, and entered the second week, we heard about Matt from time to time. Occasionally, I heard his voice myself. Other pilots said they heard him early in the morning, while I heard him at night, and he even showed up at planning meetings around midnight. So when was he sleeping, I wondered? Or was he sleeping at all?

Well into the second week of non-stop operations, we became bogged down by bad weather. A cold front had moved in accompanied by low ceilings and constant rain. It was miserable, from what I remember. You just wanted to stay in the sleeping bag to pass the time and try to stay warm. Even though we were in Louisiana, it was only mid-March and it had not yet warmed up. At about midday, one day, I thought I might swing by the operations tent to see what was happening before heading to the mess tent for a bacon sandwich. I peered out of my tent flap and looked up the hill towards the operations area to try and gauge the weather. It was cold and damp with a penetrating drizzle, and fog was partially obscuring visibility.

As I stared towards the ops area, trying to decide whether I could get away with just a flight jacket or would have to don rain gear, I saw a soldier silhouetted against the top of the hill around 100 metres away. It was definitely some poor infantry guy; his M16 assault rifle was slung ranger-style and he was hunched over from fatigue. Something about that shape was definitely familiar though; did I know that poor slob? I snatched up my rain jacket and hat, and started up the hill. The whole time, as I sloshed and splashed closer to the hunched figure, he didn't move, except to bring a rain-soaked cigarette up to his lips. This guy was so wasted, he was actually trying to smoke it. As I reached him, I realised who it was: "Matt! What the hell are you doing standing out here in the rain?" He didn't move; he didn't even acknowledge me but just continued to stare blankly straight ahead. I noticed that he had no rain gear on at all, only his rain-soaked BDUs. As I walked up to within a metre of him, he brought the drenched cigarette up to his lips again and took another long, pointless smokeless draw.

"Matt! Hey, man, are you OK?" I asked, realising that I was looking at one of the worst cases of fatigue I had ever seen. As he lowered his cigarette in an arc, a rivulet of water drained from his helmet, along his shoulder, down his arm and along his hand to the cigarette. He didn't even look at me, but just mumbled quietly, "Don", before going through the pointless ritual of raising, attempting to smoke and lowering the cigarette again. As the cigarette reached the bottom of its arc of travel, he said emphatically, "My life sucks!"

The guy was beyond tired and was probably hypothermic, I realised. He was definitely delusional. As he continued with the pointless ritual, several other officers arrived and took an interest in Matt and me and our 'conversation'. Matt wasn't even blinking. His face was coated with a mixture of mud and camouflage green and black, which had spread over his neck, collar and sleeves. He continued: "My foxhole is filled with water."

Whenever I tell this story, which I have done many times since that memorable day, it always comes out as somewhat hilarious. However, for Matt, on that day, it certainly wasn't. Realising he had reached his physical limits, we grabbed our waning friend, and walked and carried him down to the female shower tent. We chose that tent because those showers always had hot water. We showered him and put him in my clothes, which were several sizes too big and made him look like a clown, then carried him over to my tent. Within a second of placing him on my cot, he was sound asleep. We left him there for hours, and he slept and slept.

The story of Matt 'finding' us and popping up in that soggy Louisiana wood reminds me of a lost dog that finally finds its way home after going astray and enduring some great ordeal. Matt had served us all well. He had gone well above and beyond anyone's expectations and had done so at great personal expense. He had proved himself to be one hell of a man and able to hang with hard men under the toughest of conditions.

No longer a soldier, Matt now flies a regional jet around the US. I often wonder if the man sitting in the comfortable, warm left seat of that Canadair cruising along at flight level 310 ever thinks back to that cold miserable day in central Louisiana? As he looks at the glass displays of that RJ, does he remember how things used to be? I hope so, because he comes from a finer time when the measure of a man did not come from the number of stripes on his epaulettes, but from raw gut-borne determination and deep rooted love for his country, his fellow soldiers and something bigger than himself. Matt's personal determination and his actions brought honour upon himself and taught more than a few of us some very important lessons about life.

Chapter 24

REMINISCING

The nose pitched up gently to around two degrees above the horizon as we started a slow climb to flight level 330. There wasn't a cloud in the sky and the air was smooth in the climb. The jet was operating like the finely-tuned machine it was designed to be, passing effortlessly through the atmosphere at .80 Mach. I selected 500 feet-per-minute climb on the autopilot control panel, punched the vertical speed button, then started to chuckle.

In my mind, I was suddenly back in the turret of my M-60 tank at Fort Knox, Kentucky, on the basic driving course, training with my friend Doug. Doug was a loveable sort of guy, in a clumsy sort of way – the kind of guy you somehow felt compelled to tease but then later felt bad for doing so. He was a fellow tank commander and a good mate. My driver had just knocked down a tree with our tank, and Doug's driver was just about to do the same thing. Back then, Doug and I were tank commanders and instructors at the US Army Armor Center, teaching young recruits and passing on our craft of dispatching enemy tanks with precision and speed. Doug had never knocked down a tree before. Doing so was strictly forbidden and Doug liked to follow the rules, so this was going to be a new experience for him, and a treat for me.

You see, I occasionally did things I wasn't supposed to. I remembered a battalion commander who chewed my butt frequently for doing so. He told me, "Harward, if I could, I would keep you locked in a glass case labelled 'BREAK IN CASE OF WAR.'"…I think he meant it as an insult but I took it as a compliment. The commander was a paper-pusher type looking for a quick star. We called guys like him 'corporate raiders', 'clerks' or 'REMFs', none of which are complimentary terms – the last of which being the least so. (Given that I have decided to keep this story clean, I shan't explain that particular acronym to those who aren't already familiar with it.)

Doug's tank approached a sizable sassafras tree at about five miles per hour but as it got close, it suddenly lurched forward. What was he doing? The fool was supposed to drive up slowly, just touch the tree and then simply push it over. His tank hit the tree so hard the tree came out of the ground roots first and toppled over the turret, falling right on top of Doug. As the scene unfolded in front of me, I began to have one of those out-of-body moments where I found myself hovering above this incredible scene, not actually participating in it but watching in disbelief. A large branch caught Doug under his arm and, as the tank moved forward, it plucked him right out of the turret! I could see the expression on his face, a wild and crazed look, he was pulled further away as the tree rolled off the still-moving tank until, finally, the electrical helmet connection pulled apart. The driver, who was oblivious to what was going on above him, just kept driving forward, leaving Doug entangled in the tree as it rolled off the back of the tank and onto the ground.

I thought about calling the driver of his tank on the radio as he drove away, but decided not to. Doug didn't seem to be hurt and the whole thing was just too funny. The last thing I remember seeing was Doug running after his tank yelling, "Stop! Stop!" as the lumbering vehicle disappeared over a hill – simply unbelievable. The way that event unfolded describes Doug in a nutshell: he always had the best of intentions, but the results of his actions were seldom what were expected.

While still savouring the humour of the thought, a voice broke in. "What's so funny?" My co-pilot was one of those tetchy types – long in education but short on common sense. Taking my time to answer, I studied the concerned look on his face and began to wonder. Perhaps he thought I was experiencing spontaneous delayed battlefield stress syndrome reactions; he'd probably read about such things in one of his psychology classes.

As we approached Ormond Beach, Florida, we were cruising at a comfortable 0.85 Mach. I noted we had twenty-four minutes to go before commencing our approach into Nassau. The weather report indicated clear skies with a slight quartering headwind. I guessed we'd get runway 09 and started doing the mental gymnastics for the landing there. That's the funny thing about being a pilot – even if you do a fabulous job for 1,200 miles, if you bounce the plane on landing at your destination, the only thing the passengers will ever remember is the lousy touchdown.

I still couldn't get Doug out of my mind and began to think about the time I taught him another lesson in modern tank warfare called 'back-scratching'. It was just another method in a long list of unauthorised techniques that were never taught in formal circles; however, it was well known amongst experienced crews and was sometimes used in combat. Being inside fifty-two tons of steel insulates you from the outside world pretty well and gives you a false sense of safety. Enemy infantry don't like tanks very much and have developed a trick of shooting small arms at them to keep their crews buttoned up (hatches closed) while someone rushes the tank, jumps aboard and attaches an explosive. The rest, as they say, is history.

To defend themselves against such tactics, tanks travel in groups of two to three and keep watch over each other as they move, always mindful of the infantry threat. Soldiers do not generally join the infantry just because they didn't make the cut for medical school. In many cases, they join because they never made it to school at all. OK, perhaps that is a bit of an exaggeration, but while we're having fun at someone else's expense, let's continue. If an unfortunate enemy soldier makes a poor choice and tries to attack one of these mighty vehicles, a nearby tank will simply rake it with machine-gun fire, quickly removing the annoying infantry attacker. This is 'back-scratching' in a nutshell.

For obvious reasons, in today's ultra-safe and politically-correct society, one would never dream of firing on another manned vehicle during training; there is just too much of a risk of injury or damage. Or that is the theory. However, the tank range at Steele, Fort Knox was – in our minds, at least – purpose-built for some unauthorised 'back-scratching' training because there happened to be one place on the range where two tanks could be out of sight of the watch tower for several minutes. The tower was where the 'safety' guy lived. He was the company kill-joy who was hand-selected to monitor every action on the range with the intention of creating some imaginary veil of safety to protect our precious tanks and tankers – as if training for war were inherently a safe activity.

I had talked to Doug over coffee during breakfast about doing a little back-scratching. He had agreed reluctantly; or rather, I had dragged him – kicking and screaming. Doug was definitely a 'stay between the lines' sort of guy and he would never do something like this without significant coercion. When it was finally our turn to go down range, as fate would have it, Doug was in lead and I was following. All the better; I was well practised in the technique but, as with the tree incident, Doug was new to this also.

When the time came to switch to a discreet frequency, we had arranged a code word only Doug and I knew and, when the time neared, I gave it. Doug met me on frequency but tried nervously to back out of our conspiracy. However, it was too late. "One-one, this is one-three. You buttoned up?" "Yes, but

we really shouldn't be doing this." Never mind, I thought; it's too late now —
here it comes.

As I peered through the sight, all I could see was a big fluffy sleeping bag
tied neatly to the infantry hand rail on the side of his turret. What a good aim
point, I thought , as I squeezed the trigger. As my bullets bounced off the turret
of Doug's tank, about a million feathers suddenly erupted in a cloud that looked
like snow. "Hey, one-three," said Doug, "that's cool. I can hear the bullets hitting
me. What does it look like from your angle?" As I looked at what was left of his
sleeping bag, I realised that the tracer rounds had set what remained of the shred-
ded mess on fire. "Hey, one-one, I'm cold (meaning 'I have stopped firing'). You
have a small fire on the side of your turret!" The hatch flew open and Doug's
helmet emerged — followed swiftly by the rest of him carrying a fire extinguisher,
which he used to put out the flames. Those in the tower apparently mistook the
cloud of feathers for smoke and called to see what was going on. "Nothing," I
lied. "Ops normal here. You okay, one-one?"

Through the sights, I saw Doug holding up his two rubber boots, which
had been stowed just behind the sleeping bag. They had suffered the same fate
as the sleeping bag and were full of holes. I returned the signal of his extended
middle finger with a polite wave from my hatch; life was good! For the next
couple of days, the other commanders laughed and poked fun at him every
time they saw him walking through the mud in his bullet-riddled boots. His
boots might have been destroyed but Doug wasn't going to let it get the better
of him; he continued wearing those boots as a sort of badge of courage. Doug
was a hard act to follow.

Back to the present. The approach and landing was, as they said in some
movie, a piece of cake. We almost caught the downwind main gear first, but I
levelled and flared at just the right time to secure a long 'squeaker' at about
the 2,000-foot mark. As we taxied clear of the active runway, we were in a good
position to witness the American Eagle just behind us. He landed on the left
main first and bounced back into the air. He came down again on the left and
then the right, and finally planted the nose. Surely those ATR turboprops
couldn't be all that difficult to land; they must have had an unlucky gust of
wind, or the person flying was inexperienced. Someone said, "Amateur" over
the tower frequency just as I was switching to ground control, and my co-pilot
and I both chuckled.

With the important phase of my flight behind me, I allowed my mind to
drift back to Doug again. To this day, I cannot explain why we made it a personal
project to corrupt Doug; I guess it just seemed to be the right thing to do at the
time. I liked Doug and we all just wanted him to push his limits a bit to learn a

little more about himself. You see, the irony in warfare of knowing when not to follow the rules is that if you are able to live and operate on the fringe, it might just give you a small advantage that might save your bacon some day.

Eventually, all our hard work with Doug paid off. Perhaps he finally gave in to all the 'training' we had given him, or maybe he just matured and came into his own. However, one story illustrates the exact moment when something in him changed.

It was lunchtime one day in mid-summer, and we were busy training yet another group of recruits. Three other sergeants and I decided to drive to the mess hall from the sub-calibre gunnery range we were teaching at that week. The evening before, we had left the tanks on the range under guard so that we could drive our cars out there the next day. Had we not done so, we would have been condemned to eating the same C-rations the recruits had to eat.

Of the four of us, Doug, another tank commander named Eddie and I all owned Jeep CJ-7s. Doug's Jeep was stock standard – just the way he purchased it and would remain that way until the end of time. Eddie's Jeep was modified slightly but always seemed to be in the body shop recovering from an endless stream of mishaps. My Jeep was extensively modified – it was lifted, had a built engine and big mud tyres, and everybody liked its nice loud exhaust. So it was my beautiful orange Jeep that we all climbed into and headed down the tank trail towards the battalion area for lunch. I was going a little too fast, which always annoyed Doug. He pointed out the twenty-five mile per hour speed limit and curtly mentioned my lifted vehicle was not as stable as a stock one. He was always complaining about things like that. So just to prove him wrong, I steered abruptly to the right, absolutely convinced that nothing bad would happen. The Jeep responded by rolling onto its side, its top and then the other side before sliding into a two-foot high pile of dust. Let me assure you: you haven't seen dust until you've seen dust that has been pulverised by huge dirt-destroying tanks for years and years – that is some really fine powdery stuff.

When we came to rest, I was hanging in my shoulder harness on the uphill side, Eddie was below me in the passenger front seat – cussing, like normal – but he was all right. Smitty, the non-Jeep-owning fourth one of us, who sat behind me, had had the amazing good sense to grab hold of a flying speaker that came loose as the Jeep rolled; otherwise, it would probably have taken one of us out. He was also OK. Only about ten percent of Doug was visible; he was almost completely buried beneath the dust the Jeep had scraped up during its rollover and slide. "Doug! Are you all right?" we yelled. As Doug's shoulder moved, Smitty, who had already unbuckled himself, began digging in the dust for Doug's seat belt. He found and released it, and pulled Doug up. Poor Doug was exactly

the same colour as the pulverised mud and only the three narrow slits of mois-
ture where his eyes and mouth were supposed to be distinguished his face.

Fortunately, apart from having eaten a mouthful of Kentucky's finest mud
mix, Doug was OK too. He smiled, wiped his eyes, looked at me and said, "Told
ya!" About that time, a basic training platoon marched up to the crash site and
halted. When the sergeant asked us what had happened. Doug, who was the
ranking guy in our dust-covered group, took a long look at me before stepping
forward. He told the sergeant what a great job the driver – me – had done in
steering to avoid a ground hog that had been standing in the road. We got the
dubious smile we expected from the sergeant, who, after establishing that none
of us seemed the worse for wear, ordered his trainees to roll the Jeep back onto
its wheels. We checked the oil, I cranked the engine and it started! We thanked
everyone and drove off quickly.

Being forced to defend me with a bold-faced lie was a crossroad event in
Doug's life. He had had two choices: he could have told the truth and seen me
suffer the punishment I deserved, or chosen, as he did, to protect his friend by
compromising his own values. He was never the same from that day on; he was
better in a strange inexplicable way. He squared up to people, seemed to have
better posture and gained confidence. As he became able to operate in the grey
zone just a little past the line, he even became able to hold me at bay. He earned
my respect and trust in a way I would never have anticipated; he was a good
solid leader, a great and loyal friend and a valuable asset to the army.

I always considered Doug to be amongst the ranks of those we describe as
unsung heroes. Later, after I left for flight school to become a pilot and an officer,
I heard about Doug from time to time, but never saw him again. Nevertheless,
thinking about him always brings a smile to my face.

Chapter 25

MEMORIAL DAY

It just happened to be Memorial Day, but in Afghanistan, it didn't seem any different from any other day. The flag outside was still flying at half-mast. I wasn't sure if it was flying that way for the guys who were killed a couple of days earlier, or perhaps someone from the previous night – I didn't want to ask.

Today, when I look at the many images on the TV or the internet of wounded soldiers and hear their heart-wrenching stories, it always conjures up similar images in my mind – images like that day in Afghanistan. I think I am always going to remember those times and events – you just don't get some things out of your head.

I remember another Memorial Day. It was a little chilly as I stood motionless in a group of several hundred men, all of us wearing our dress green uniforms with highly polished boots and maroon berets. People went up to a podium one by one; most dressed in suits, some in uniforms. They talked about this and that, the things they remembered about the *person* who was a soldier, and whom they obviously loved dearly.

Leaves stirred as flags fluttered in the breeze, but the hundreds of men stood motionless as if frozen. As people spoke, every word resounded in our ears, as we, too, remembered. It was easier to stare straight ahead with our eyes fixed on infinity, but I could not; I stared at a row of women and children seated opposite my formation. Some of them looked at the people speaking and tried to present an appearance of dignified grace. One woman was clutching her children who were crying.

As the speakers' words ended, the rustling of the leaves gave way to the sound of approaching helicopters, but the seated women did not look up. As the helicopters – a formation of MH-6 'Little Birds' – flew directly overhead in a perfect 'V', one of them pitched up and banked gracefully away from the formation. I watched it briefly and then glanced at one of the women, who was dressed in black. Her head and eyes followed that single aircraft as it turned – seemingly toward heaven. I believe, in her mind's eye, she was seeing her husband on his last flight as he pitched up, never to return. I had known him; he was a heroic 'Night Stalker', and he would never be coming home.

I remember another time, in a Chicago bar, attending a wake. The parents of the fallen soldier and his surviving brother and sister asked me to join them in a private room; I was there to bury their son the next day. After inviting me to sit, they asked me just two questions. "Can you tell us how he died…and why?" I knew the answer to the first part easily enough. He had been piloting his MH-60 Blackhawk helicopter when it had crashed in Iraq during a mission. But how was I to answer their second question?

I considered my answer carefully; I knew that whatever I said would be imprinted in their memories forever. I answered slowly and looked them straight in their eyes. "He died because he was a soldier. He had no concern for his personal safety – only for the successful completion of his mission. He died because someone has to take the fight to our enemy; someone has to risk it all; someone has to be selfless enough to do what needs to be done when others will not – and when that happens, someone almost always pays with his life."

His sister, who lived out west, told us that on the day her brother had died – and before she had been told of his death – she had been hiking in the mountains. As she had stopped at a scenic lookout and stared at the sky, a lone eagle flew towards her and circled directly above her for a while before flying on. She said that at that moment she had felt something she could not explain – but I think I know what it was, and I think that deep down inside, she did too.

My wife Kathy got a chance to see a little of the price soldiers pay on the battlefield. While visiting me in Landstuhl Army Hospital in Germany, she saw many torn and wounded soldiers. I watched her as they came hobbling by wearing casts, bandages and steel wires holding their broken limbs together. The way she looked and sometimes covered her mouth said it all. You just don't see that sort of stuff in normal hospitals; at least I haven't seen it.

Oddly enough, when listening to those broken guys, the common message one always seems to hear is their desire to get back into the fight. They feel that they have let their buddies down by having been shot, or blown up, or whatever. Many people might call them crazy or shell-shocked, or describe them as suffering from some sort of delayed combat stress, I don't know. I call them patriots – the best their country has – and I think of them as heroes.

My Dad, mentioned before, a soft-spoken survivor of the war against Nazi Germany and the Axis powers – was just such a hero. As a very young man, he piloted his B-17G to war, where he took many lives by delivering his deadly bombs to their targets, and where he was also shot up and crashed. He didn't talk about it much, but he understood war on a personal level. He knew people didn't just get shot cleanly and fall down unconscious. He knew that it was not that simple. He knew that no matter how awful it felt, he had to climb back into that cockpit day after day and keep doing his job.

I remember my Dad giving me combat advice – a son who had just finished a second combat tour. I'm sure he was trying to give me pointers that might save my bacon in the future, or maybe he felt I had reached a level of maturity to handle such things. I hold these memories close to my heart. They, and many others like them have become the very bedrock of my being. That foundation, and a healthy dose of spiritual faith, is all I need to know who created me, who I am, where I come from, what I stand for, and what I believe in.

No hint of political correctness will ever be part of me. There is not, and never can be any honour in being politically correct. It is just a polite way of lying and I'll have none of it. Being politically correct has got us to where we, as a society, currently find ourselves with an identity crisis. It is not politically correct to say there are religious groups that hate us. It is not politically correct to admit that we have to do something about it – and I don't mean debate it endlessly in the marble and granite halls of Washington. It is still not politically correct to tell the truth about what is going on in Afghanistan or, more to the point, what the war might really be about.

I had written a paragraph describing my opinions on the problems we face in the current war zones, but I decided to delete it. As I've said, I am not political, and I don't want to mix the memories of honourable soldiers with the lying babble of the politically correct, so I'll just leave it alone. Those of you who read this know what I am talking about anyway; you are like me. You are the reason we are over here; you are the people of the free world. I pray you remain strong and your numbers multiply because we need you as much as you need us.

Not long ago, I flew a fairly high-ranking dignitary around. What a stark contrast there was between 'them and us' as he and his entourage climbed aboard my helicopter. They wore jackets, pressed trousers and polished shoes, and had an air of calm disregard about them. We wore dusty uniforms festooned with the weapons and tools of war that were integral parts of our daily lives. When the principal climbed aboard he had to push aside an M4 carbine that was attached by a chord to the roof near the door, and his associates seemed mildly annoyed by the 'clutter' of medical rucksacks and weapons secured around the aircraft's interior.

The two combat medics crewing my ship made their assessments of our passengers. Which one of our passengers would panic if we took fire? Could they be trusted not to go stumbling into the tail rotor? Which one/s would we have to keep a close eye on?

Scotty, the other pilot, and I were similarly dressed. We had on one-piece flight suits, combat boots and flight helmets. I wore an American flag attached to a Velcro patch on the back of my helmet. Scotty wore Oakley boots of the kind originally designed for our special forces, and which we jokingly referred to as 'over-stocked dot-com boots', because of the trendy oval affixed to their sides. Both of us had our kit set up in such a way that we would have been ready to fight the minute we hit the ground in the event we had our helicopter shot out from under us. Scotty's aeroscout background and my special ops experience dovetailed nicely together. Both of us knew the deal and what to do if things got ugly. When one was flying, the other was always ready to take over if the guy on the controls took a round. I flew with a double magazine locked in and the weapon on safe. Practice had taught me to place a finger alongside the trigger housing with my thumb on the safety, which I knew to push twice to enable a three-round burst of automatic fire when I squeezed the trigger.

Our vests were set up so that under blindfold conditions we knew exactly where everything was located. On the bottom right were a total of six thirty-round magazines. To their left was a single thirty-round 'night' mag loaded with pure tracers. Tracer bullets leave a red trail that is easy to see and helps to aim automatic fire; I would have used these to mark an enemy position at night if I were shot down so that our gunners could have delivered 3,000 rounds a minute to the point where the tracers were striking.

Next to that was my medical kit. It had a long tab that made it easy to grab with slippery hands; pull the tab left, and the first thing inside was a bag of 'quick clot', a substance which, when poured on a wound, can stop bleeding and save a life. Next to that, under my left arm, was my survival radio and a small flashlight. Above that were three M9s, nine-mm pistol magazines which, had I ever had to use them, would have meant I was having an extraordinarily bad day. Then there were two 'catch all' pouches. In one, I kept my personal GPS, a signalling mirror, and matches. In the other, I carried more bandages and some gum; had to have gum! Finally there was the one-handed tourniquet, which we practised applying from time to time.

Our guests in the back were yelling at one another over the beating of the blades and the scream of the turbine engine as we picked up, did a pedal turn and accelerated over the taxiway to take off. We flew with no doors at all, so the

VIPs must have felt a little bit out of their element; no quiet and comfortable interiors here. We flew that way to allow anybody on board to have good fields of view and of fire. I climbed and watched our formation spread out around me. We had a gunship accelerating past us on the left, and two birds with security types on board tucked in right behind us. We were going to a local hot spot where an IED had exploded causing casualties just the day before. My plan was to swing wide to the west, away from the city, while the gun bird approached at 500 feet from the east. I noted his position, started my turn in and dropped to 300 feet. As the gun bird completed its first clearing turn over the objective, I maintained 300 feet and accelerated. The gun bird reported all clear and I began banking right and left so that no one on the ground could get a good shot at us. I glanced over my shoulder at the principal and his aides, who seemed oblivious to the whole thing. Whether they realised it or not, their lives were totally in my hands for the next two to three minutes.

Having the gunship circle had telegraphed our plan to the enemy, and they were definitely there. Whether or not they would behave was a 50/50 proposition, but I was prepared for a gunfight anyway. I headed in the general direction of our landing site, but banking right and left the whole time, never making it obvious where I was going to land. As I drew closer, I hoped that from the ground, it would have appeared as though I was doing a low pass by the landing area. At the last minute, I cranked the aircraft to the left, reduced power and descended quickly, flaring as we sank over the twelve-foot high blast wall protecting the compound. I can't help wondering what the VIP in the back thought after a ride like that, but it didn't matter – my job had been to get him there in one piece. In doing so, I had to place a multi-million-dollar helicopter in a known shooting gallery and exposed Americans to great danger. I'll bet the folks in the back didn't have a clue what was really happening – which delineated the differences between their lives and ours.

I disliked doing any VIP work, especially in a combat zone, but it really is part of the job these days. Embedded press, gawkers, elected officials, you name it. Whoever they were, I always made it clear to our passengers that if the shooting started, it would not be a pleasant ride, but would be all about getting them out alive and unscratched if possible. I didn't want there to be any confusion in their minds about the differences between flying in a combat helicopter and a commercial airline flight. When I piloted a jet airliner, it was all about comfort and convenience for the passengers to ensure they kept coming back and swiping the plastic. Not in a war zone though, where, once on board an aircraft, it was always possible one might never come back.

When we went back to pick up our VIP and his associates, I approached the site differently. As I lifted off, I stayed low and accelerated quickly to gain air-speed. Then, I pitched the nose up with the power still in and was rewarded with a rapid climb. I knew we were being watched. The chances were that amongst the ranks of people working in the compound there might well have been Taliban sympathisers who had given away our position. The odds were that they were more likely to shoot at us with small arms like AKs, so altitude was our best friend. In Vietnam, Huey pilots flew at around 1,500–2,000 feet to avoid small arms fire. Now, decades later, we do exactly the same thing except when a mission calls for us to fly lower. Within a couple of minutes we were at 3,000 or more feet and enjoying a much cooler temperature and a scenic view.

Flying at altitude could be a little disconcerting for passengers in the back; some of their seats faced outwards only inches from the opening where the door would normally be. Passengers in these seats had to physically hold their legs in if they didn't want them blown about by the 100 plus mile per hour windblast. I'll bet that as our passengers looked down to see nothing below them for several thousand feet, they probably had serious thoughts about how dependable their seat belts were. Thankfully, none of our VIPs fell out of the helicopter and with another mission ended safely, it was time to get some chow, unwind, and turn on the tube. With the fan in my room spinning on low, I killed the lights and drifted off to sleep as a dinosaur documentary played on Discovery. I knew the next day would bring its own new challenges, but it was time to let my mind drift to dreams of family, home, and happy days to come.

Chapter 26

FAREWELL TO TWO
BRAVE MARINES

I was waiting at the terminal today for my flight. I was inside the old TLS build-ing down near base operations. The TLS building is a veritable fortress made of stone, brick and concrete with walls possibly six feet thick and, seemingly im-pervious, one might think, to harm from above or below. Apparently, many members of the Taliban must have believed the building offered safety and shelter from US attacks in the last stages of the war in 2001. Unfortunately for them, the name subsequently coined for the building – to which the acronym TLS refers – is the 'Taliban's Last Stand'. Rather than providing the shelter the Taliban expected, the walls of the TLS served merely to magnify the over-pressure of the exploding bomb that hit the building killing all of its occupants. When the US Army occupied the TLS soon afterwards, they repaired most of its structure except the ceiling, which still bears black sooty stains from the fires that burned there. The blackened ceiling serves as a reminder that this country was taken by force and claimed the lives of many of our young men as well as the lives of our enemies. We soldiers often do things like that; we leave behind small reminders of battles fought, sacrifices made and lives lost.

The massive roof of the TLS building is supported by a series of intercon-nected archways, each of which forms a hallway of sorts, and I was sitting in one of those hallways.

Its walls, which had been painted some time after US forces had occupied it were now adorned with little messages left behind by departing warriors and I amused myself by reading them. The writer of one of them was going back to Waco, Texas, another referred to the Royal Marines. Some of the scribbling was funny, some hateful and some hopeful, while others farewelled friends who would not be going home. All seemed to telegraph warnings of the danger that lay beyond the walls.

The design of the TLS building provides a natural cooling effect, which I found far preferable to the oven-like roasting heat just outside. The view from that tunnel-like hallway looks out towards the flight line where my 'freedom jet' would soon be parking. I had been on that ramp literally hundreds of times, either embarking or disembarking from an aeroplane or taxiing in there myself to pick someone up.

When I first glanced outside, everything seemed normal – but this feeling was deceptive. I first noticed the C-17 parked at a forty-five-degree angle with its nose facing outward and its rear cargo ramp lowered and facing towards me. That, in itself, was not particular noteworthy, but it should have been a clue as to what was about to happen. Not too much later, I was again staring outside as I anxiously awaited the arrival of the DC-9 that would carry me and a number of my colleagues away from Kandahar to begin the journeys to our respective homes and safety in the outside world.

For no other reason than that I wanted to stretch my legs, I got up and walked outside. As I glanced towards the C-17, I noticed a set of speakers set up on the tarmac on either side of the rear of the aircraft; now that was definitely not normal. It was then that I realised what was about to happen and a glance to my left confirmed it. A long line comprising two columns of US Marines was walking slowly and methodically towards the ramp of that plane. They moved in perfect unison, as if they were one, each marine's leg lifting at exactly the same moment as 100 others. With one column on each side of the ramp as they approached the plane, the marines formed a corridor that extended perhaps 150 feet from the rear of the plane. The marines halted and, as if driven by a common set of gears, both columns turned to face inwards towards each other before moving to the position of 'parade rest'. Done in complete silence, it was a spectacle to behold.

Another column of troops – this time, US Army soldiers, perhaps several hundred strong – moved into a position outside the column of marines…then another and another.

I brought myself to parade rest, while many of the civilians stood just behind the fence began to remove their hats. Columns of soldiers from a dozen different nations moved into a grid pattern, all facing inwards toward the vacant corridor. British and Australian soldiers swung their arms back and forth in an exaggerated fashion as they joined smaller formations of Bulgarians, Romanians, Danish, Germans and Dutch troops and marched into place. Next, moving forwards slowly in line abreast with absolute precision, came a colour guard of four marines. Two of the marines carried flags; one carried an American flag, while another carried the red flag of the Marine Corps. The two other marines flanking their colleagues carried M4 carbines at their shoulders. Slowly, and deliberately, the men marched directly to a point adjacent to the open corridor. I drew myself to attention. The sun was burning the top of my head, and sweat ran off my head and legs, but I didn't move.

A sergeant major called the assemblage to attention: "Pre-sent Arms!" I watched several thousand right hands being raised slowly in salutes. The salute to honour a fallen soldier is not presented in the normal fashion; it is performed very slowly, as if painful to deliver – which, I suppose, it is.

As we all stood there in the hot desert air, a French Mirage fighter, fresh from a sortie, landed and popped its landing 'chute. As the aircraft turned off the runway onto the parallel taxiway adjacent to the ceremony, the pilot must have realised what was happening, as he immediately throttled back and came to a respectful stop while the ceremony proceeded.

At the sergeant major's call of "Or-der-Arms!" those thousands of saluting right arms descended slowly in unison back into position: alongside the body, hands cupped, touching the trouser seam. As a panel truck pulled slowly into view, two squads of six marines each moved into position. The truck stopped and its aft ramp lowered hydraulically. The marine chaplain began to speak. His words echoed amongst the buildings as he spoke of the young men who had been taken and how they were much too young to have paid such a high price. Several thousand people scarcely breathed as they watched and listened and no one uttered a sound. As the chaplain spoke, the only other sound I could hear was the flapping of the worn US flag on a nearby flagpole on the TLS building.

As the first of two flag-draped coffins appeared out of the back of the truck, the first squad of six marines moved into position, three on each side, facing the box. The colours of the US flag completely covered the container, in stark contrast to the windblown dusty brown colour of the concrete ramp. It was as if the thirteen red and white stripes and the fifty bright white stars against the flag's field of blue had been added to a dreary black and white photograph.

The marines lifted the coffin onto their shoulders and turned simultaneously to face the ramp of the C-17. They carried the coffin above their heads and began to march slowly in unison toward the ramp. The second coffin was quickly hoisted and it, too, passed slowly up that long, sombre corridor of men and women. The marine pallbearers stood resolutely motionless for a couple of minutes as the coffins were laid together in the back of the plane. With the coffins secured, the bearers turned in silence and marched back down the line to join their fellow marines.

I don't know how long I stood at attention as the soldier inside me mourned the terrible loss of those two young men. I considered the stark contrast of our two very different realities: these two young men were going home to their final resting place and would never roam the earth again. At the same time, here I was, a much older man, waiting for a flight to carry me home safely to my family. I had seen much war; this had been their first. My family waited anxiously for me to get home so we could enjoy some fun family adventures together. The families of those two boys would have tragically different expectations and they would be stricken with grief as they awaited the return of their loved ones in very different circumstances, knowing only that their lives would never be the same.

As I stood there at attention, through the corner of my eye I saw a couple of civilians looking at me; KBR contractors, I think, who were probably going home for some R&R. No doubt they were wondering why I was standing at attention. Clearly, they had no military backgrounds or they would have stood as I did, honouring our dead as any soldier would. However, they did nothing wrong – what they did was fine, and it was all they knew to do.

The ramp of the C-17 began rising and then stopped about one-third shut, as if to give the two warriors inside one last brief glimpse of the land that had taken their earthly lives; it was hugely symbolic to me. This foreign land, to which those two brave warriors had come to fight enemies of the entire free world, was the last they would ever set foot upon. The dusty, tortured desert paths they trod here were their last contact with the world they knew. In a moment of horrible violence, their lives were taken from them here. I wondered if they even knew when the fateful moment came.

The procession started to move away from the grey-winged monster as, one by one, its engines started. As the C-17 taxied slowly out of view, I finally relaxed and turned to walk back inside. I realised I was almost alone and most of the other people had already walked silently away. How long I stood there, I don't know. But I could not simply turn back. I remained standing there until that USAF monster raced past me on the runway and climbed skyward. As it did, I remembered the words of the poem, High Flight, by John Gillespie Magee Jr.

> *Oh, I have slipped the surly bonds of earth*
> *And danced the skies on laughter-silvered wings;*
> *Sunward I've climbed, and joined the tumbling mirth*

Of sun-split clouds – and done a hundred things
You have not dreamed of – wheeled and soared and swung
High in the sunlit silence. Hov'ring there,
I've chased the shouting wind along, and flung
My eager craft through footless halls of air.

Up, up the long, delirious, burning blue
I've topped the wind-swept heights with easy grace.
Where never lark, or even eagle flew –
And, while with silent, lifting mind I've trod
The high, untrespassed sanctity of space
Put out my hand, and touched the face of God.

Two fallen heroes of my country were on their final journey home. A journey I know neither of them anticipated, nor would have chosen deliberately. Nevertheless, in the fashion of true warriors, they had chosen. In choosing to wear the uniforms of US Marines, they knew it would someday put them in harm's way. Oblivious to the dangers, they came thousands of miles to fight an evil scourge and, in doing so, paid the price for my freedom, and that of my family and friends, and the civilised world, with their courageous young lives.

Chapter 27

EARLY MORNING
COFFEE AND TALIBAN

The Tim Horton plastic coffee mug – filled with a very early morning mixture closely akin to actual coffee – felt reassuring in my hands as I sat silently in the briefing room. Even though there was hardly a sound, people occupied every seat while many others sat on the floor or leaned against the walls. Many of them also held or sipped their early morning java as we all sat awaiting the launch decision. It was so early that you couldn't really call it morning at all; that daily event was still hours away. No sir, this was still night, but just far enough on the other side of midnight to somehow qualify.

We had pre-flighted and loaded our gear into our heavily-laden aircraft the previous day, which really was just eight or nine hours earlier. Because of the particulars of this mission, most of the warriors gathered here had, just like me, probably had little sleep. Instead, they would have spent the hours of darkness in and out of a dream state with their minds working through the phases of the raid we were going to fly today. I was still rehearsing it as I sat there in that room. Pinned around the walls was an array of charts, aerial photographs, timetables, photographs of the target building, evasion plans, load plans and a host of other mission-related documents. Front and centre was the all-important weather forecast in which every block denoted a favourable number; visibility was forecast to be more than ten miles, ceilings were non-existent and the wind speed would be mercifully low enough that the probability it would generate a dust storm was virtually nil.

The factors had miraculously come together to make it all happen. The ground mission commander and the air mission commander were in another room making the final call as to whether to launch or to go back to bed and wait for another day. The biggest factor for me was the weather; I just hate flying if the weather guesser – after throwing his whalebones and reading his tea leaves – predicts it will be 'just above minimums'. Undoubtedly it will always be above minimums somewhere in Asia I guess, but as fate always seems to have it, in most of the places where I'm actually going to be flying, it usually ends up being well below minimums.

The other piece of this all-important pie was that our target had to be at the place we were going to in order to make the mission a go. We already knew there was a lot of illegal activity at the destination, so I wondered why we didn't just go there and blow the whole thing up anyway. Then, if he wasn't there, when we found out where he was later, we could go in and blow that place up too. I mean why not? It's like zero-too-early in the morning and we're all dressed up anyway. Let's get out there and wreck something!

Two grave faces entered the room, Joe (name changed to protect the innocent and all that) and the ground commander. Today, I was going to be flying in the right seat, which meant I would actually be doing most of the flying, but Joe was the aircraft commander and the air mission commander. When our eyes met he gave me a small hint of a smile. That was all I needed to know. Joe was a warrior just like me; he liked a good fight and to hit the enemy where it hurt, no matter what the circumstances. Joe's smile told me that we were going to get to play today…the mission was a go. The ground commander told us that the person we had on the ground was saying all the right things and that the target individual had been sighted in the village. The weather was good, as Joe ran down the various numbers. He looked at his wristwatch and told us that H-hour would be 0620.

Once the first part of the process – the decision as to whether to actually carry out a mission – has been made, the second part is to establish a detailed timeline. H-hour is a very specific time. Once it is established, we plug it into the timeline and work backwards all the way to the 'commo' (communications equipment) check, which is when we test the radios in the aircraft just before line-up and take-off. Before that, of course, we must walk out to the aircraft, strap in and crank up. That piece of the timeline is flexible for the most part; some folks bound out to the aircraft, strap in, pull the starter trigger and, *viola* – they're ready to go. That would not be the case with me, and certainly not with Joe; he had the added burden of having to run the whole aerial mission, which had a lot of variables. I liked it because, firstly, I would know what was going on and secondly, because I would be flying almost the whole day.

Looking at the timeline and doing the mental arithmetic, I could see we had little time left and really needed to get out to the aircraft right away. Joe looked at me through sleepy eyes. "You ready for this?" he asked. "Yep. Let's get out there and win a couple of air medals."

Outside the building where we had assembled it was still dark and the air was very cool. It might not be much fun to walk around in the cold, unable to see anything in the dark, but it is very good for heavily-loaded helicopters which need every bit of cool dense air to propel themselves off the ground and lift their cumbersome loads.

As we joined the aircrews making their way to their various aircraft, I used my Gerber aluminium flashlight to illuminate a smallish circle on the ground in front of me. The helicopters were parked on concrete but between them and us was a strip of dirt with a big ditch in it. I knew roughly where the ditch was, as various other flashlights ahead of us suddenly descended then reappeared. One flashlight appeared to fly forwards before stopping abruptly, then followed a rearwards arc as its holder fell backwards into the ditch after foolishly trying to jump it. Ah; young men and their youthful exuberance. Joe chuckled when it happened then said: "Lost one already."

Joe was an interesting character. He and I had an uneasy relationship that went back a little more than a year. He was not an American, but was a dammed good combat pilot in his own right. The poor guy had never actually ever flown in a peaceful setting; he became a pilot when his country was at war and learned how to fly during that war. Along the way, he met my boys and began a lifelong relationship with the US military. As a result, he got to know important people who recognised his value. When the programme we were involved in began in Kandahar a couple of years earlier, he was chosen to join the team because of all his experience.

I came to like him almost immediately. He was soft spoken and sometimes had difficulties with English but he never turned down a mission. He could have and earned just as much money, which was considerable, had he chosen not to fly, but he never did. At one stage, he and I both had the opportunity to be the lead pilot for a group which was to be sent north – the very group in which I was about to fly this mission as a member today. I chose to stay down south in Kandahar where I thought the fight really was rather than go to what I saw as a 'sleepy hollow' up north. I never regretted my decision, and Joe was doing a remarkable job. He was a good lead pilot and tactician and was getting the job done. However, he was always mindful of where I had come from in my army days and I think it made him uncomfortable, so there was a slight air of uneasiness between us.

Today we would be flying the gun bird. And not just any gun bird, but the one tasked with providing direct support over the target building. Next to us on the ramp was the CSAR ship and its medics who we hoped would not be necessary. Those guys only go to work when things go badly, you see. They were stone-cold professionals and it always felt good knowing they were nearby. They would be somewhere around the target but just out of harm's way. After all, you don't want the doctor to get hurt when you need him the most.

Joe and I took some time to set up our helmets with our night vision goggles. I plugged in the battery switch and flipped the switch to 'Primary'. Both tubes glowed green; a quick flip to the alternate battery pack gave the same positive result. I hung the HGU-56 lightweight aviation helmet on a light and walked down the right side of the aircraft – where I immediately bumped into the barrels of the GAU-17 mini gun. Mike, our burly gunner, asked if I was OK. A super trooper in all respects, Mike is a gentle giant of a man – quiet and caring while simultaneously being a pure warrior through and through. He had personally trained most of our gunners and, as he was on the right side of the aircraft, he would be the first to engage should we need to during the mission.

The ground troops were elsewhere on the ramp. They would be flying aboard larger and less manoeuvrable Mi-8 helicopters. Our job was to escort them in and provide watch for them while they were on approach or landing. Once the troops were on the ground, the Mi-8s would fly to a loiter area or return for fuel while we provided cover for the ground forces they had just disgorged.

I met Joe at the back of the aircraft. He, like me, was an older pilot and even though we had both pre-flighted the day before, we were still giving the bird one last walk around just to be sure. It was an unnecessary step, but we did it out of habit. He smiled and so did I. We walked back to our respective sides and climbed in. As I struggled with the right shoulder strap, which had somehow become tangled behind me, Mike handed it to me and I buckled in. His silhouette looked like the incredible hulk; the guy was just enormous without so much as an ounce of fat on him. He had been a US Marine and never stopped looking the part. "You ready Mike?" I asked him. "Yes Sir, ready as I'll ever be. Let's start this pig and turn some jet gas into noise." The latter phrase was mine; Mike repeated it out of recognition that I was now a member of the team – and also because he was having some early morning fun with me. "OK, Mike, let's git 'er done."

Around five minutes before commo-check time the Hueys began to crank up. The growing whine of numerous spooling engines was both a comfort and a signal that it all was about to happen. With six sets of huge rotor blades turning at a steady 324 rpm, the ramp was vibrating with the power of it. At exactly the appointed time, right down to the second, Joe keyed the mic and said, "One-one on one, one-one on two, one-one on three," and so forth, as he keyed through the various radios. As the other aircraft did the same in sequence, he marked off on a kneeboard chart those he could hear, and any he could not. Communications is important as you can imagine and so far on this very early morning, it was all good.

"Flight, this is lead. Switch to set two…set two." The call came from the flight lead aircraft and not from us. Although we were the mission command ship, the job of flight lead fell to another aircraft. It would be his job to get all of us to the target on time. He had just asked us all to switch to the assigned frequencies in line two of the communications page of our mission packets. I switched the radios and heard lead calling ground control for the taxi. One by one, the lights came on and we repositioned to the area of the taxiway we would use for our take-off run. Each of the aircraft called ready as they completed their engine performance tests.

"Roger that, flight. I have all aircraft ready for take-off. Switch to set three…set three." As we settled into our position in the line-up, we made our final pre-take-off checks then set our exterior lighting to the prescribed setting. The lights are adjustable and switchable and are used to communicate your status to the other aircrews silently. "Tower, this is Delta one-one flight. Requesting take-off to the east; we have information Sierra." "Delta one-one flight, wind is three two zero at five knots. Cleared for take-off; report cleared to the east."

Six birds now began their take-off runs while hovering just barely above the ground. Even though the air was cool and dense, the birds were loaded to the gills and the pilots were nursing every ounce of lift from the helicopters' big metal rotor blades. Joe called, "eighty-seven, ninety, ninety-two, ninety-three, ninety-five; holding ninety-five (the magic number of 100 percent must not be exceeded), eighty-eight, eighty-five…We're flying."

When first tilted forward, the Huey will take just a tad more power. At around sixteen to twenty-four knots forward speed, the aircraft will give three or four solid 'whump, whump, whump' sounds and then suddenly spring into flight. This phenomenon is called 'effective translational lift' and occurs when the whole rotor system finally receives clean undisturbed air. Up until that time, the rotor is 'eating' its own vortices, which kill lift and obviously make the engine work much harder.

We climbed out briskly up to our initial cruising altitude. Even though it was still night, looking under the goggles rewarded us with a view of Kabul. The city is quite spread out with some taller buildings to the south and is ringed by very tall mountains in all directions. Unfortunately, that fact keeps stale stagnant air overhead and today was no exception. Below us was a pall of smoke hovering perhaps 100 feet over the city. Apparently living in Kabul in the winter is equivalent to smoking a pack of cigarettes a day!

At the appointed spot, lead directed another change of frequency. "Flight, push set five…set five." Now we were on our internal frequencies where we heard some chatter from the flight of Mi-8s somewhere up ahead. Since all the aircraft would be refuelling, and the Russian Mils took much longer to do so, the mission planners had wisely decided to allow them to use their faster cruise speed to get to the FARP sooner so that they might be finished before we arrived. It almost worked out that way, as they were still sipping fuel fifty minutes later when we arrived at the FARP. They cleared the US Army-manned refuelling points and we hovered into position. After taking on the pre-planned amount of fuel, we moved away to a rocky spot where we rolled the throttles down to idle. We had flown through BMNT (before morning nautical twilight − a point in time at which the sun appears twelve degrees below the actual horizon). This time is important because night vision goggles become increasingly less effective as the amount of daylight increases with the rising sun. For both operational and safety reasons, we had decided to give it a little time to get brighter and launch without the NVGs to fly the short distance remaining to the target.

Down near the Pakistani border amongst the mountains lie many small villages. One of those was currently being observed from above and would soon be the focus of a lot of attention. H-hour − the time the first Mi-8 was due to land − was fast approaching; our take-off time from the FARP had almost arrived. I rolled the throttle up to full rotor RPM and lightened the aircraft on the skids with a slight pull of the collective. With less fuel aboard than we had earlier, the bird was ready to go flying. Lead took off first followed by Chalk 2. I increased power slightly and pushed forward on the cyclic; we were up and away and I tucked in behind lead in a staggered right formation. The Mi-8s called off as well and the whole airborne juggernaut was up and away towards what we hoped was an unsuspecting target.

Intelligence had located a cache of weapons and ammunition as well as a decent quantity of drugs. Today, they were all neatly packaged within four walls, with the added bonus that the guy who actually owned all of it was

present there as well. As a political comment, please don't tell me the Taliban
are some sort of freedom fighters or religious warriors; they are simply crim-
inals dealing in a prolific drug trade that also finances some of their military
operations. Considering that other nearby nations quietly donate weapons to
the Taliban to use against us anyway, I don't buy the idea that the drugs are
some kind of 'necessary evil' they use in desperation.

The terrain in the target area rose in steps that seemed to support the massive mountains further to the south and east. On about the third step up, several
thousand feet above sea level, the village we were assaulting had just come
into view. The tension rose and I felt my heartbeat increasing. The SAR bird
peeled off and went high. I could see the Mi–8s approaching from our left and
Joe was carefully studying the photograph and scanning for the house. Our
first job was to circle the LZ ahead of the Mi–8s and suppress any fire the
landing aircraft might be taking. As soon as the last Mi–8 cleared the LZ we
had to immediately establish a circle around the suspect house and attempt to
stop anyone from fleeing that location. People who run from the target are
called 'squinters'.

We accelerated to arrive above the approaching Mi–8 and pulled into a
nice right orbit at about 500 feet just as he flared and landed. Immediately,
soldiers came racing out of it, running from its lowered rear ramp.

In seconds, the soldiers were all off and the aircraft quickly took off. Another Mi–8 flared and landed in the same spot, while another landed in a different spot. The lone Mi–8's troops served as a blocking force along the
village's only road. In seconds, the town was becoming ours. The blocking
force spread out, sealing off the road, while the assault force moved directly
towards the objective. By now, I was circling the target house. There was no
question that we had the right one; the match was perfect. With all the noise
caused by the helicopters landing, people began coming out of their homes
to see what was going on. We picked up two squinters who ran out of a back
gate and down a hill toward a creek and a field of tall crops. I circled aggres-
sively close to them, hoping they would shoot at us. Had they done so, Mike
would have smoked them in a New York minute (which is not very long) and
they would not have got away.

They did not shoot, and we radioed their position to a ground unit that
broke away to pursue them. We watched as the two groups met and our guys
zipped up the squinters. We made it back overhead the objective compound
just as explosives ripped the front gate to pieces and the assault force rushed
inside. Code words flew over the battle frequency one after another as we
scrambled to make sense of it. The assault troops wrapped up the prime target

and found all sorts of goodies inside. Then, another call stated that they found a tunnel! Outside in the streets, a couple of mobs began to form. I pointed the nose at one and started a dive directly toward them. They got the message and dispersed, running all over the place in the opposite direction. It might have looked cool at the time, but I don't like scaring people nearly to death. However, more importantly, I didn't want any of our guys to get so much as a scratch.

With a quick flick of the cyclic, we were back over the compound in a screaming tight turn. Joe looked over at me with his mouth curled in a slight smile. "Having fun, are we?" "Ooooh yes!" Back over the compound, I transferred the controls to Joe. The next thirty minutes or so of ground activity gave Joe a chance to have some fun flying as well. We continued to circle, being careful to vary our flight path, turn points, and altitude constantly. The chatter on the battle frequency was all good. Things were going according to our plan. The assault guys were finding mines, RPGs, dope, heavy machine guns, and the kitchen sink. It was turning out to be a bad day for our T-ban buddies down below.

The ground commander gave the order to wire it all with explosives, and the guys in the tunnel and in the compound did exactly that. Meanwhile, a group of very unhappy folks wearing nylon zip-tie wrist bracelets were marched toward the LZ. A radio call brought the first Mi-8 back and it picked up the prisoners and some of the assault team members. Joe made a pass or two at the gathering crowds and they got the message. Next came the general extraction call; a time when our guys have to perform a dangerous movement back to the pickup point. It is a time of increased danger. Even though the primary objective and its people might have been neutralised, there are always a few who get away. It would be about now that they would be likely to pull out the trusty old AK-47 and attempt to drill us full of holes. Joe transferred the controls back to me again and we covered the movement of our guys as well as we could.

I heard my favourite warning being given: "Five minutes. Repeat: five minutes." That call meant someone had just lit the fuse on all those explosives and, in exactly five minutes, the whole place was going to go ka-boom! This is a very critical time. We had to get our people out, while simultaneously trying to keep all the villagers away from the hazard area. As the last Mi-8 took off, one of our Hueys landed close to the compound to extract the demo and security guys and then lifted off. I flew directly over him in the opposite direction to watch for anyone who might try to shoot him on take-off. With everyone off the ground and moving out of the area, with about a minute to spare, I pulled in power and cyclic and climbed to about 1,500 feet over the compound. A short time later, the inside of the compound – specifically, the southern half of the house – erupted into a black cloud. At first, I couldn't see if the blast was effective, as the dust cloud rolled outwards in all directions. Had it not been, we were to pour mini-gun fire into the building in an attempt to destroy it.

However, after a couple of passes, it was obvious there would be no need for any additional gunplay. The house was definitely destroyed. There was a hole in the ground where the tunnel had probably connected to the house and it looked as though nothing useable would be coming out of that hole again, ever. I took one last look before pulling around in a standard rate turn towards the tail end of the formation and towards home. The CSAR bird came zipping down the slope to my left and joined up with us. He had been parked somewhere up there on a nearby rocky slope watching and waiting. Joe spoke the final code word, which indicated the target had been destroyed.

All in all, it had been a pretty good day. We had taken out an important Taliban leader – or rather, a drug lord – let's not mince words here. The stash of drugs and weapons had also been destroyed and the operation effectively shut down. We had lost no one and neither had the enemy. Ahead of us waited another hot cup of coffee and a proper breakfast; not a bad day at all.

Chapter 28

STRANGERS IN
THE NIGHT

Here are some thoughts on green air and dust. The other night, our mission went on well after sunset. Our flight route took us across a desert area – a place known locally as the Red Desert – for about fifty minutes. The hemispherical illumination from the moon, which was nearly overhead, was pretty good at seventy-seven percent. Illumination from the moon and stars is very useful when flying around in black air with NVGs. We were using one of the latest generations of NVGs, or just goggles as we call them. When looking through them at a dark scene, everything appears in varying shades of green.

On this particular mission, I was the AMC for a flight that took us across plenty of uninhabited space, but ultimately ended up at a southern Afghan city – a place where the Taliban occasionally played. Crossing from the Panjwai valley and its fields of beautiful-looking poppy plants into the featureless desert was a tactical choice that made sense. The valley provides plenty of contrast with the winding shallow river, sporadic fields and farms. The great contrast makes it easy to see terra firma and is thus easy to fly in. However, it is home to plenty of people who would like to see us harmed. Out in the desert, the ground shows less texture when viewed through the goggles than areas where there is vegetation. The fact that the sky and sand there are pretty much all the same shade through the goggles introduces its own danger, as it is difficult to see the ground. Thus, we had the choice: fly through the valley with its great contrast and easy flying – but danger from ground fire – or take the route through the potentially hazardous flying conditions of the desert that offered us relative safety from Taliban guns. Someday I want my decisions to be no more complicated than… chicken, or beef?

As we flew deeper into the desert, Mike was at the controls while I made radio calls on the area tactical control centre frequency to get an idea what was out there that night. Mike was maintaining a good altitude and about a quarter of a mile trail behind lead, in what is known as a combat cruise formation. In such a formation, the trail ships simply keep lead in sight while manoeuvring from side to side to use the terrain to best advantage for masking. Mike seemed to be completely comfortable with all of it; he is a strong and proven combat pilot, a veteran of the Bosnian campaign and more than a year in Afghanistan.

Looking ahead, I began to notice it was becoming increasingly difficult to see lead. Looking to the left, I realised I could no longer see into the desert, while to the right, the hills were also becoming difficult to pick out. We had flown right into a dust storm without even seeing it. I got a call from lead saying he still had the mountains to our right. I took the hint and asked him to turn right to pick up the valley to take our chances.

On the southern bank of the river, which is the start of the Panjwai valley, are a few sparsely scattered Bedouin camps. They look harmless enough but I do not trust them at all – for good reason. Probably ninety-nine percent of them are just nomadic tribal people living a medieval lifestyle but sometimes, they shelter something much deadlier. I remembered back to the opening night of the first Desert war; I had been in the cockpit of an Army MH-47 Chinook helicopter. Our route towards our staging area to cover the raids on a southern Iraqi airfield took us right by just such a Bedouin camp. Within seconds of passing it, we had been fired upon by three surface-to-air missiles, which led to the loss of our aircraft. It's a long story, and I won't bore anyone with it, but it sure taught me the lesson that when you are in Indian country with your game face on, don't trust anybody who didn't attend the same briefing as you did.

That experience continues to circulate through my grey matter on a semi-regular basis, so it is never far away when I fly by those innocent-looking low black tents in the middle of nowhere. We crossed several clusters of those tents while transiting the area between our base and the destination but thankfully, on this night, all was quiet. That's the weird thing about this place. One day all is well in a given spot, the next day somebody gets shot there, so you learn to never let your guard down.

The visibility improved steadily as we pushed on westwards until finally we had pretty clear skies and perhaps twenty miles of visibility. Approaching the city where lead had to land and drop off a passenger, I thought about the best way to cover his approach with the gunship we were flying. Mike and I talked about it for a while before deciding to position ourselves slightly behind and above the landing aircraft. Sometimes, the gun bird might sprint in ahead of the formation to clear the landing area, trying to spot any snipers, roof top gunners, or suspicious vehicles that might be dangerous. At other times, it stays in formation. It is wise not to create any habits in combat. Whatever you do today can't be the same thing you do tomorrow; you must never be predictable.

Digressing briefly: I remember flying convoy cover in Baghdad in a MD-530F 'Little Bird' in 2005. We flew the helicopter without doors − much the same as we do our Hueys in Afghanistan − in order to give us a better view and, if necessary, get off a shot with our personal weapons. We were circling a high-rise building just across the river and slightly north of the US Embassy. As we spiralled down from rooftop height, we were looking for any signs of snipers in the building, which sits right beside a bridge known to aviators as 'Bridge One'. On that bridge next to the building we were circling was an Iraqi National Guard checkpoint. As I looked down at a pickup truck stopped at the checkpoint almost directly below our aircraft, the vehicle suddenly exploded. We were literally right in the blast. I didn't hear a thing and I don't remember it throwing us around. One second, the sky was clear; the very next instant we were surrounded by a boiling black dust cloud that smelled of ammonia. Someone had waited until we were right overhead before detonating that VBIED (vehicle-borne improvised explosive device) in the hopes of bagging a helicopter.

Another concern of mine was trying not to be seen at night. The enemy can hear us coming, but can't actually see us most of the time. I learned that lesson during the invasion of Panama while flying a seal team into Padilla − a small airport on the shoreline in the middle of Panama City where Panama's military governor, Noriega, kept a personal jet. As we approached, tracer fire from the ground streaked high above the rotor system. I had thought that by flying an MH-47 only twenty feet above the water at around 140 knots in the black of the night that we were in real danger. However, as we approached the runway, I noticed the glowing tracer fireflies weren't getting any closer. It dawned on me that whoever was shooting at us couldn't actually see us, but was firing at the sound, which has a tendency to bounce off walls and other obstructions in a way that totally confused listening onlookers.

Back to my story. Had the moon been too bright, we could have been seen with the naked eye. Had we gone in too low then the belly of the aircraft would have appeared as a glowing orb; too high, and my gunners would not have been able to identify targets properly or engage accurately had they needed to. (Imag-

ine the effect of spraying mini-gun fire into a densely-populated city.) Considering those factors, we selected an appropriate altitude and followed lead in. He
made a straight-in approach up a long strip of dirt in the centre of the city. As
soon as he cleared the compound walls, we bugged out to the south to orbit
over a sparsely populated area nearby. All went well, lead departed and we linked
up. Minutes later, job done, both aircraft were cleared to the north and proceeded
to a nearby firebase.

The army special forces guys at the firebase fed us almost every day at their
modest mess hall and we had got to know them quite well. We did them favours
whenever we could, and this was a perfect opportunity to give them a helping
hand. They had asked us to give them an over-flight whenever we were in the
area at night because experience has proved that a simple over-flight by a helicopter can prevent an impending attack. Our enemies know they cannot win
against aircraft so they often choose to call it a night and go home if they are in
the area. Just a few nights earlier, that firebase had been attacked, and a sustained
fight ensued for several hours. Taliban fighters overran one of the guard towers
on the base perimeter, which they had held for a short time before finding their
way, suddenly, to paradise, courtesy of the US Army.

As we approached the firebase, I didn't want to make a call inbound, because
it would have given anyone who might have been monitoring the frequency
valuable seconds to set up on us. However, I was mindful that the base frequently
lobbed quite a few 105-mm artillery shells out in all directions. Those tubes had
fired several thousand rounds in just the previous few months! On the one hand,
I would, sort of, like to know if I were heading for the same piece of sky as an
outbound 105-mm projectile. But frankly, I consider the chance of that to be
slim, so we just trust that the gunners will hear us coming and hold their fire
until they no longer hear us in the area.

I told lead to give them an inside and then a wider outside sweep, while we
flew off to their right side. A battle was going on nearby to the north; someone
was getting hammered up in the Sangin valley. Tracer fire bounced into the air
and artillery fell with magnesium flares hanging 2,000 feet in the air illuminating
the ground below. On the sector air coordination frequency I could hear fighter
pilots talking. Someone was air refuelling, while another pair was being vectored
onto a target.

It was nice to watch from a distance, but after an hour-and-a-half of fun, it
was time to go home. I called lead and told them to turn east for Kandahar.
Once we left the combat area, it was quiet enough during a 'relaxing' flight
back to base that as I thought of my wife and home, I began humming Leaving
on a Jet Plane – an old John Denver, and Peter, Paul, and Mary tune.

It has become a habit of mine to sing those old tunes and it has a funny side when I do it deliberately. Almost every time I go out to the aircraft to pre-flight it and get ready for a mission, I start singing a song. Not just any song, but one that is seldom heard, and it has to have a catchy tune. One day, I had Mr. Sinatra's famous tune, Strangers in the Night stuck in my head.

"Strangers in the night, exchanging glances
Wond'ring in the night
What were the chances we'd be sharing love
Before the night was through."

I kept humming or singing it continuously while the refuellers topped off the auxiliary fuel tanks, the gunners loaded ammo in the cans, the mechanics cleaned the windows and checked over the birds, and the other pilots and I set up our goggles on our helmets and organised our cockpits. It wasn't long before I heard one of the gunners, then one of the other pilots starting to hum those same familiar bars.

Every once in a while throughout our subsequent mission down to Spin Buldak and back, I heard that tune over the intercom. When we arrived back at Kandahar after the mission, we taxied up our dusty ramp, did our two-minute cool down and I rolled the throttle off. Standing just beside me on the ramp as I pulled my helmet off my head, was Greg, our avionics mechanic. What do you think he was doing? What else? He was singing Strangers in the Night! He realised as soon as I looked at him and smiled that I had him.

"You!" he said. "You stuck that song in my head. I've been singing it ever since you left!" I just smiled and chuckled; I'd got another one and it had been pretty easy.

Since then, many a hardened warrior has succumbed to the likes of John Denver's Country Roads, Styx's Babe, Jim Croce's Operator and America's Horse with no Name. I had even victimised my oldest son Don in the same fashion during our long distance runs together. Don, I know you're smiling this very second.

Chapter 29

QUIET
PROFESSIONALS

The community calls them the quiet professionals. Once, I was one of them and sometimes, I still have the privilege to continue to serve with them. Some call them 'operators'; they are the men and women of the green berets, special forces, seals, special air services, force recon – and a plethora of other names. Some of them are placed in various levels unmentioned outside of 'the community'. Whether they come from the army, navy, marines, air force – or other countries – they are all the same at heart and are cut from the same bolt of cloth.

As a former army pilot, I might have been considered to be green, since green is more or less the army's colour – although US Marines might take exception. We might have called you 'blue' if you came from another branch of the military, or maybe even a 'purple suiter'. The latter, more recent, term refers to how, on a given mission, there might be people from various branches doing separate but very important missions as part of some larger operation. And the mixing of their various uniform colours might combine to form purple. Although these missions have been many, you will seldom hear of them. Only some gain notoriety, such as the one in which a US Army Chinook that was carrying a team of US Navy Seals was downed in the hills of Afghanistan.

Our quiet professionals are well known by our enemies because of the frequency with which they meet. However, these same good guy forces are not all that well known by their own countrymen. Given the hunger for information by over-active news media that constantly seeks to plaster operationally-sensitive information all over the TV, the efforts by the military's elite forces to remain in the shadows must be appreciated.

You might have seen Hollywood interpretations of some special operations missions but the chances of their bearing any resemblance to reality is very slim. Most of what I have seen coming out of Hollywood is neither technically correct, nor a true representation of what really happened. No one from within the community really gives a hoot as to whether the media gets it right anyway, since we know they will lie about it or spin it to fit their story in the end. People without honour do things like that without a second thought. Oddly enough, there is a good side to the Hollywood version of 'reality'. While Hollywood keeps folks entertained by some made up or over dramatised story, the quiet professionals continue to practice their deadly trade unnoticed.

Following Mogadishu – or more to the point, the amazing battle that was fought by army rangers and others who were there – we pulled our assets back home to our shores and licked our wounds. As a Chinook pilot at the time, I was not there; there was no place for me, as the powers that be did not see fit to use that airframe. I suppose that if the largish Chinooks had been there, possibly with me at the controls, I probably would not be writing about it today. Instead, it was the Little Bird and Blackhawk guys who were sent out on an alert that some did not return from. Shortly after everyone got back to the States there was a very low-key memorial service held at a classified location in the US. I was lucky enough to attend having flown a Chinook full of our people to pay their respects to the many fallen and wounded.

The large auditorium in which the service was held was packed with many dignitaries from various branches of the government and the military. It was so packed, in fact, that I had to view it from a satellite room and watch it on a TV monitor. That was OK by me; I was wearing my flight suit, and I never felt all that comfortable with Washington-types anyway.

The first thing I noted was that neither our then president, nor the vice president, were in attendance. I suppose there were more pressing matters that required their attention; and that is as kind as I will ever be about them not being there. The room was a virtual who's who of some of the most powerful people of America. When the glad-handing amongst the people in that large assemblage was finally over, the dull roar died off and the audience fell silent and took their seats.

The ceremony began with a prayer from an army chaplain. Next, the unit commander gave the order to perform a roll call. If you have never seen that spectacle before, then you have missed a very solemn and humbling experience, as few ceremonies have the power to draw one in as this one does. It is a poignant and moving way in which we honour our fellow fallen warriors. The sergeant major stood and began calling names alphabetically (I have changed some of the names here out of respect for their families):

"Allen!"
"Here, Sergeant Major!"
"Campbell!"
"Here, Sergeant Major!"
"Gordon!" This time, there was no reply – just a meaningful silence.
"Gordon. Master Sergeant Gordon!" queried the sergeant major once again, only to be answered once again by a painful silence.

I felt it in my gut as I feel it right now, and I saw tissues wiping tear-filled eyes throughout that gathering. The sergeant major turned to face the commander and said in a much softer voice, "Sir, Sergeant Gordon is missing, he has fallen in battle." After another brief silence, the roll call continued. Several more times the soldiers being hailed did not answer the calls. And so it went for some time until all of the names had been called.

At the end, you could have heard a pin drop. The deafening silence was broken by a bump and a shuffling sound as a wounded soldier started to make his way forward toward the podium. We heard the drop of his foot followed by the dragging of his supporting crutch, then the sound of him shifting his weight to repeat the awkward movement. It took quite some time for him to finally reach the stage area. He obviously should have been hospitalised, but there was no way a man of honour such as he would not have been there for his buddies. One arm was in a sling and the other was bandaged. He had a cast on one leg, and his head was bandaged. The leg without a cast was also bandaged and he was obviously in a great deal of pain. A thousand sets of eyes were fixed on the man as he stood there in front of everyone.

There was a small stage set up which was no more than about two or three inches higher than the aisle. It looked to have been built recently and hastily with 2 x 4s and simple plywood sheeting. The soldier tried to lift his leg the two inches to climb up onto the stage, but he could not; the spectacle had everyone in tears. One of the dignitaries stood slowly, walked over to the wounded soldier and carefully lifted the man's leg and placed it on the stage. He then lifted the soldier and helped him crest the small rise. I felt the power and richness of that moment. This was true respect and humility so thick you could have cut it with a knife. Here was one of the world's most powerful men obviously just as smitten by what he saw as the rest of us and clearly overcome with compassion for the wounded warrior and the sacrifices he had made. Not once did the soldier call out or wince in pain. Just as he had silently borne the burden of having to go to a foreign land to fight for his nation, now he simply bore his suffering in silence. This man and those he sought to honour were, quite literally, the quiet professionals – unknown to all but a few.

This particular quiet professional, a special forces soldier, spoke softly about his friend for a few moments. Not only did his words convey the pain he felt for his great loss but they also gave a real sense of the characters of both the speaker and his friend. The soldier said nothing negative at all – no looking to blame anyone, no call for any investigation, and no veiled threats. These hallowed halls, where the personal sacrifices bought and paid for with the blood of these patriots were commemorated, were a place for great integrity, honour, respect and courage.

I felt and observed it there as I have in many other places around the world: the distinctive aura of the warrior. It is a statement they make without making a statement. It is a palpable feeling that something very different and very powerful is present. Over the years, I have come to recognise and know it quite well, and it is something I have the eyes for. Their ways are quiet and subtle – things you might miss entirely if you blink. If you ever take the time to engage a returning warrior, you might discover just a hint of it for yourself. Look for the one who is silent and introspective, with that 'thousand-yard stare' I have written about before. If, when you first approach him, he acts startled, as if you just woke him from a vivid dream, it is because you just did.

I suppose I should comment on how this warrior aura comes to be in the first place. You see, you cannot come back from war and immediately fit back into the comfortable world at home in the US or other countries. You feel as if you no longer belong and, for some reason, you don't feel as if you deserve to be home once again – it is as if you have to earn the right to be back. You feel guilty that you are able to sit there in air-conditioned comfort while your brothers are still enduring the heat and the dust in the deadly streets of Afghanistan or Iraq.

It is impossibly hard to just turn it off as you would with a light switch. For example, today's returned warrior seeing a dead animal lying at the side of the road might well swerve into the far lane, half expecting the animal to explode suddenly; this is because dead carcasses are among terrorists' favourite hiding places for IEDs. I suppose part of the mystique which makes up the persona of the quiet professional is borne of their experiences.

Experiencing loss and witnessing suffering also probably contributes to the make-up of the quiet professional. The need to suppress feelings and emotions and continue, no matter what, is another thread I am sure you will find woven in that warrior fabric somewhere.

Although I have seen the suffering myself, I guess I must have tucked it away somewhere in my soul as well. One day, a few years back, I was reminded of it all when my wife spent some time with me in a hospital, briefly mentioned earlier. Watching her allowed me to see another human try to come to terms with the sacrifices made by our young people on the battlefields of faraway lands.

I had been sent to an army evacuation hospital in Germany after suffering a non-combat related injury in Afghanistan. My wife Kathy, unbelievably, made it over there on the second day. I was in my room when she arrived fresh off the flight from Cincinnati. It was a good time, a growing time for both of us. Initially, she was very concerned about me but as I healed and I began to move around, we began taking walks in the long hospital corridors. There, we saw other wounded warriors lying, or sitting, or walking around. The Landstuhl Army Hospital is another hallowed place for many of our nation's heroes. More than once I saw my wife's horrified reaction as she saw heinously-wounded soldiers making their way along or lying in their beds.

On one occasion, we went down to one of the vendors at the hospital snack bar for a sandwich. As we sat up near the counter, chatting and enjoying our food, a lone soldier walked in on a single crutch. His opposite arm was raised and wired together with one of those external steel skeleton things that hold badly broken bones together. I saw Kathy cover her mouth again as the soldier made his way up to the counter to order a meal. The vendor placed the soldier's burger and fries on a tray and the soldier fumbled for some cash. I walked over to him, paid for his meal and invited him to join us at our table. He thanked me and sat down clumsily. I got him a drink and we both watched as he tried to eat the sandwich with his good hand. Kathy's eyes filled with tears as he struggled and dropped food all over. I helped him hold the food so he could eat it and we sat there in silence for some time.

When he had finished eating, I pointed to his arm and asked him what had happened. He looked at us and began to speak – beginning by calling me "Sir", as he explained what had happened to him. He told us that he had been on a foot patrol in Iraq when he saw what he thought was a freshly buried IED ahead on the road. As he raised his M4 carbine and looked through its three-power, ACOG optical sight, he saw a wire coming out of the dirt, which he traced over to a building and then up to a second story apartment. Evidently, someone must have seen him following the wire with his rifle sight and, as he followed the wire scanning for a target, an enemy bullet entered his hand between two of his fingers. It travelled its horribly destructive path along the length of his forearm and exited from where his elbow had been. Kathy was weeping quietly and I looked at the mound of bandage surrounding his steel stabilised elbow.

What he said next was remarkable – although I have heard it many times before it always has the same effect on me. He said, "Sir, I have to get back to my squad. Those guys are one man short without me; I'm not carrying my load." Before us sat a young man who was obviously fighting for the use of his arm, which I later learned he was in danger of losing. However, this did not matter to him as much as the thought of letting his comrades down. Not once did he complain about the pain, the loss of his arm, or his radically changed future – not once. He did not complain because honourable men care more for their brothers than they do for themselves. He was just an ordinary infantry soldier, not one of special operations' quiet professionals, but the same warrior spirit was clearly alive in this man.

I have seen the same spirit in the flying business as well. During the infamous Mogadishu battle I spoke of earlier, one of our pilots was wounded by enemy fire. Despite the pain and loss of blood from his wounds, he continued to fly his heavily-damaged gunship to provide rocket and mini-gun fire to support the trapped rangers.

I don't know what forces conspire to make men like these. I don't know any magical formula or particular training that can so change a man. Perhaps some are born with it; perhaps others are somehow changed by experiences. Perhaps the change takes place slowly over many days of painful route marches, sleepless nights and tired feet. I don't know, and I'll wager good money that no one else does either, but maybe it's a little bit of all of it and something else too. I can't say, but I do know that I'm dammed glad we have such men and I'm fairly certain that we would not have our nation without them.

When I used to fly out of Washington LZ, adjacent to the US Embassy in Baghdad years ago, the gunner's wall locker in the hangar from which we flew had a quote, paraphrased from George Orwell, written on one of the doors that sums it all up:

> *We sleep safe in our beds at night*
> *Because rough men stand ready*
> *To visit violence upon*
> *Those who would do us harm.*

EPILOGUE

AN AVIATOR'S PRAYER
BY DONALD HARWARD

The enemy lurks everywhere
Five hundred feet below
In the shadows, caves, and trenches
And yet I always have to go

Their desire it is, to end my life
And drive us from this land
But something else is at work here
Guided by his mighty hand

Our lives, they are not ours to have
But owned, by another one
We try to do what we think is right
And pray to his only son

Even as a single ship
In formation, I have flown
The angels always have been there
Protecting us alone

I fling my craft through mountain pass
And over desert plain
They shoot at us with RPGs
His protection still remains

Though our aircraft may be armoured
And have deadly weapons too
The prayers of our fellow countrymen
Are what really got us through

Those prayers, they are what really count
And not some armoured plate
They lift us up before his throne
And he decides our fate

They view us as invaders,
We occupy their land
They believe we are all infidels
And have some other plan

But truth be known, it is not that
I really do not know
I simply fly my rotorcraft
Over the ground so low

Another day has come to me
And more missions to be flown
I'll bend a knee before I fly
My prayers to him are known

I have no time for politics
The decisions have been made
I'll strap in again, and start the thing
And spin that rotor blade

For God is with me, this I know
Even in this dusty place
There is nowhere that I can go
Where I'm not covered by his grace

So fear be gone, that devil's trick
That waits at silent bay
To take away the joy and awe
Of this, my father's day

The take-off check, away we go
Within this flying thing
Our confidence is strong today
We fly upon God's wing

Much as we do most every day
We'll fly off into the air
Knowing that we ride upon
The assurance of your prayer.

INDEX